Dolls' House Dolls
1850-1900
Magdalena Byfield

Contents

5
1850-1860
15
1860-1870
31
1870-1880
37
1880-1890
47
1890-1900
63
All-Bisque

Copyright © 1977
Living Dolls Publications Ltd
P.O. Box 2
Enfield
Middlesex

All Rights Reserved. No part of this publication may be
reproduced, stored in a retrieval system, or transmitted, in
any form or by any means, electronic, mechanical,
photocopying, recording or otherwise, without the prior
permission of Living Dolls Publications Ltd.

ISBN O 905956 OO 1

Foreword

Such are the changes that a few years bring about,
and so do things pass away like a tale that is told.

Dickens

It is an interesting phenomenon that generations have always rebelled against that which has gone immediately before. There is an inevitable period of contempt for the fashions in their widest sense, of ones immediate forebears. It seems that a duration of time must elapse and we must cut loose all connections in order to assess with a detached eye the values of an earlier age. Collectors of dolls' houses are perhaps alone in evaluating and indeed trying to preserve, that which is just fading into the recesses of memory. They aim to keep alive the slender thread which leads us back in time through the generations. To retrace a path that links grandparents with great-grandparents — to freeze a moment within a miniature complex.

The collecting of miniatura is by no means new and much is owed to collectors past and present for preserving for us these miniature artifacts, for not only are they extremely appealing, but pay gracious attention to fashion and all its outward manifestations of social behaviour. Not least in silent eloquence is the miniature or dolls' house doll. These were manufactured in large numbers throughout the latter half of the nineteenth century to take their place in the miniature interiors. It is with the dolls of this period that this book is concerned. They were not play dolls in the same sense as their larger counterparts, but were as indispensable a part of a fully equipped miniature household as was the kitchen range. As the vogue in furniture and trappings changed so the doll altered in shape, dress and coiffeur to resemble the prevailing ideal. Trammels in dress were contrived to advertise the leisured status but this did not apply only to the higher classes for menials too wore their distinguishing marks. The dolls' house doll followed the all-conquering mode and whether male or female, adult or child, faithfully testifies to the fashion of its day and to its social position.

The exact dating of any dolls other than those accompanied by contemporary documentation is a precarious business. To commit oneself to a definite period in time without a doll's full history is courageous if foolhardy. Even where dolls carry a manufacturer's mark and one knows the dates during which this dollmaker was active, a certain amount of guesswork must still be confessed to. Makers often continued in business for several decades and while adding new innovations to their products also retained and continued to use their earlier moulds. To further confuse the issue, moulds are known to have been withdrawn for periods and then re-introduced at a later date.

With miniature dolls there is a total absence of markings — except in very rare instances — and one must contrive by other means to arrive at a "possible" date. Inevitably the most valuable clues are obtained from manner of dress, style of coiffeur and type of footwear, but here too, alas, there are pitfalls for the unwary. Apart from the most obvious contingency of the doll having been re-dressed to keep abreast of fashion (as were their miniature residences which frequently have numerous layers of wallpaper to testify to this fact), fashion did not reach out its tentacles as widely as is commonly supposed. Many people wore modified versions of current modes which are not easily recognisable as belonging to the age. During the 1870's and 80's for instance, the bustle like all fashion novelties provoked a good deal of reproof and many held the vogue in contempt and never wore it at all!

While contemporary fashion illustrations might lead one to suppose that a particular style was universally worn in a given period, this holds no more true than present-day fashion periodicals reflect what the average woman is wearing now. Also with the less efficient communications of the previous century even the most fashion-conscious person might only become aware of a new vagary when it had already fallen from favour at the fashion front. To further vex us is the Victorian custom of changing ones clothes several times during the course of a single day — each garment being applicable to a different purpose. This practice applied to men as well as women and also servants. There were given modes for "breakfast wear" and clothes for the late morning varied according to whether one was going a short distance on foot or out in a carriage. There were "afternoon" or "afternoon ceremony" dresses, "tea gowns" and formal or informal "evening dress' and a turbulent array of correct accessories and outergarments to go with each outfit.

Miniature dolls were usually dressed at home and often reflect this chaos of styles. When they were dressed to represent actual members of a family and household their value as fashion documents is undeniable and a sense of life and reality is added to an already beguiling toy.

This book is concerned with dolls' house dolls in Europe. Germany is their most likely country of origin as she was the undisputed leader in the field of toymaking, with France a close second, while other European countries are also thought to have made some dolls. Provenance is virtually an impossibility in the absence of markings. In their fashions they reflect versions of modes influenced no doubt by France, England and Italy. It should always be borne in mind that the nursery seamstress was to a very large degree restricted by economy of means. Dolls clothes were made of scraps left over by the family dressmaker and this must have resulted in a good deal of frustration while being an excellent training for inventiveness. Little wonder that Victorian children were superlative needlewomen, exercising a patience which to our modern culture is almost incomprehensible.

Mode of footwear is of help in arriving at an earliest possible date for a doll. Most dolls' house dolls had their shoes moulded on and painted, sometimes with great elaboration. A gradual rising of the heel began after 1855 until by the mid-70's high heels were general. It is therefore reasonable to assume that a doll with heels to her shoes cannot be earlier than 1855, though correspondingly it should not be concluded that flat heels represent a doll prior to this period, for as already stated, dollmakers continued using moulds concurrently with more up to date models and again not everyone wore heels simply because they were "de rigeur"! Styles of hair share the same ambiguity as footwear — one can only arrive at an earliest possible date.

One aspect of dating is sadly the deterioration in manufacture of a product that has been on the market for some time. This is often evident when two identical models with a lapse of time between their respective productions are placed side by side. The colouring, texture and detail have often become slipshod and nebulous. Initially the doll had been produced with an eye to catching a market. There is a crispness and high quality in these archetypes which is demonstrable. Once the doll had become an established seller production was stepped up and the aesthetic aspect was sacrificed to mass production.

The popularity of sport escalated rapidly after the 1870's and inevitably brought about a healthier complexion. In dolls reflecting this period the white "skin" and rouged cheeks gradually give way to a more naturalistic treatment of skin colouring, though curiously this was in many instances confined to the shoulder-head only — the lower limbs remaining untinted.

In spite of the slender and often confusing evidence available I hope that this book can to some small degree widen the interest of dolls' house collectors in these wholly delightful residents who were an integral part of the playhouse and who can sketch for us a piece of history that encapsulates their era with the same magical charm as the miniature furnishings.

The compilation of this book has been arranged in chronological order of the fashions the dolls wear rather than their probable dates of manufacture, except in the case of dolls without clothing or in fancy dress, where hairstyles are given primary consideration. The book has not been set out as an exhaustive study of this specialised subject, but is rather in the nature of a small offering from one collector to others. The work is based on personal experience and if any of the views stated are at varience with those of the reader, I humbly beg they sift and extract that which they feel to be applicable.

M.B. 1976

1850~1860

1850~1860

Dutch doll

The wooden doll is recorded since earliest times but by 1850 the peg-wooden or Dutch Doll was being succeeded in popularity by dolls' house dolls made in other mediums. The term Dutch doll is a corruption of "Deutsch" doll as the greatest numbers came from the Black Forest area of Germany where the lush pine woods made their production an economical commodity.

Fig 1 displayed with her extensive wardrobe is of a design which in the mid-nineteenth century had barely altered in fifty years. 2in high (5cm) she is of turned and carved wood with a painted and varnished head, shoulders and limbs. The head is spherical without any features in relief. She wears a severe centre parted hairstyle with a small carved topknot at the back of the head and grey spit curls on the cheeks. The hair is painted black with a grey perimeter softening the outline. The eyes are black dots with grey eye lines and eyebrows. The mouth is very small and bright red and there are strong blush marks on the cheeks. The lower arms terminate in stumps with no attempt at representing hands but the feet wear carved flat shoes of bright green. She is peg jointed at the shoulders, elbows, hips and knees.

Her handmade clothes are masterpieces of miniature dressmaking and reflect the importance in which such skills were held. Leisure activities for the Victorian child were preferably sedentary and didactic in order to conform to the prevailing concept of refinement. Physical exertion was discouraged in an age when reticence and decorum were the hallmark of good behaviour. In a mid-nineteenth century book "The Little Girl's Own Book" the author Mrs Child writes: "The dressing of dolls is a useful as well as a pleasant employment for little girls. If they are careful about small gowns, caps and spencers, it will tend to make them ingenious about their own dresses when they are older."

This beautifully made 18-piece miniature wardrobe consists of: A pair of crochet cotton shawls, one blue and white and one beige and white, both made to fasten at the neck with cotton drawstrings of blue and beige respectively. A white cotton cape decorated with feather stitching and edged with scallops of needle-edged lace has dark blue ribbon ties at the neck and a matching bonnet with a single tuck decorated with the same stitch and lace. A second bonnet also of white cotton has three rows of drawstrings and feather stitching around the brim. A third is quite plain except for three microscopic tucks. All the bonnets are made to be tied under the chin. There are four petticoats. One is of blue wool feather stitched with white and with a white waistband. Two are of white cotton with drawstrings at the waist, two tucks and a row of decorative stitching. A fourth more elaborate petticoat has a single tuck with two rows of feather stitching and lace trim at the hem. Each of the petticoats increases a little in size on the one to go beneath it so that they can all be worn without any irregular bunching to form the desired fullness beneath the crinoline dress.

The dress is of rose velvet trimmed at the sleeves and off-the-shoulder neckline with scallops of needle made lace and yellow feather stitch embroidery. There are also two rows of embroidery at the hem of the skirt. Drawstrings at the neckline and waist ensure an accurate fit. The matching mantle is edged with a band of white silk ribbon decorated with the same yellow ornamental stitch and with yellow fine braid ties at the neck. The neckline is trimmed with a coarser version of the scalloped needle lace. Finally there are three aprons. One of black and one of dark blue cotton and one of green velvet. The green and blue aprons have yellow embroidery and cotton ties while the black has pink decoration with black ribbon ties.

To our twentieth century eyes the infliction of such a task on young hands and the considerable eye strain this will have imposed takes on the proportions of an endurance test! But we can never fully comprehend the reactions and appreciations of people living in a period other than our own. It may well be that these painstaking occupations were richly rewarding to the children who made them and that our modern society is the poorer for this lack of acquaintance with such creative tests of discipline.

Dutch doll

1850-1860

Fig 1. 2in (5cm). Peg-wooden or Dutch Doll, displayed with her extensive miniature wardrobe. (Author's Collection)

1850-1860 # Peg-jointed doll

Fig 2. 4in (10cm). A fine example of a China Limb Doll. The body is of turned and carved wood, peg-jointed at the shoulders, elbows, hips and knees. The shoulder-head and lower arms of glazed porcelain are tinted a realistic flesh colour, the lower legs, also of glazed porcelain are untinted to simulate white stockings with coral coloured moulded slippers. (Author's Collection)

Fig 2a,b,c is 4in (10cm) high. She came without clothing and now wears a dress of the 1870's. Figs b and c display the remarkable versatility of movement of the peg jointed body design. It must have been a most satisfying toy as the extreme variations of attitude will have lent realism to any dolls' house interior.

The shoulder head and lower arms of glazed porcelain are tinted a realistic flesh colour. The features are painted with a high degree of artistic skill. Light blue eyes with black eyelines, red lid lines and black eyebrows. The nostrils and inner eye corners have red dots and the lips are painted rose red with a central dark red line. There are strong blushmarks

Peg-jointed doll

1850-1860

on the cheeks. The moulded black hair with centre parting is arranged in a style fashionable throughout the 1840's and 50's. Uniform ringlets of this length were termed "heartbreakers". The shoulders are attached to the body by pegging through three holes, two in front and one behind. The body is of turned and carved wood, peg jointed at the shoulders, elbows, hips and knees. The lower legs also of glazed porcelain are untinted to simulate white stockings with coral coloured moulded slippers with rounded toes. There is a slight indication of heels and the soles are creamy white. The doll's hands are modelled with the right hand clenched and the left open.

1850-1860 'Penny doll' and Boy doll

Fig 3 is a 1½in (4cm) all-wax "penny doll" of ca 1802 but dressed at an unspecified date suggesting the mid-nineteenth century by the style and materials used. The doll is without articulation and seam marks show it was poured into a two-piece mould. A break at the feet reveals that it is hollow and the wax very thin.

Hair, eyes and mouth are painted but extremely worn. The doll wears a hand-sewn, off-the-shoulder yellow silk dress without sleeves and with a lace over-dress. A yellow ribbon is tied at the waist and her bonnet and additional dresses are of hand-sewn white cotton, minutely tucked. All of the five extra dresses are sleeveless and two have embroidered hems. The needlework appears to be the product of a talented amateur in her childhood. Nineteenth century documentation photographed with the doll reads: "A doll made about 1802 with clothes to put on. Nancy Leslie."

Fig 3. 1½in (4cm). All wax 'Penny Doll'. Nineteenth century documentation photographed with the doll reads: 'A doll made about 1802 with clothes to put on. Nancy Leslie.' (Author's Collection)

Fig 4. This rare white glazed porcelain shoulder head of a boy has black moulded windswept hair indicated by brush strokes round the face. There are no comb marks. His light blue eyes have black eyelines and thick black brows. His mouth is light orange and the cheeks have blushmarks. The dolls' lower legs are of turned wood, gessoed and painted with flat black ankle boots and lemon soles. His arms are white bisque. The head is attached to a brown hand-sewn cloth body by stitching through single sew holes front and back. His fanciful costume is without realism and cannot be hinged to any given historical period. This is not an infrequent occurrence among miniature dolls and its roots may lie in the great popularity of fancy dress parties both for children and adults throughout the nineteenth century. Roccoco modes were much favoured for these functions as were ethnic costumes.

Collectors are sometimes puzzled and misled by the appearance of these styles which must in effect be classified as theatrical or fancy dress, often the creations of young imaginative minds based on impressions and unimpeded by self-conscious attention to correct detail.

Fig 4. 5½in (14cm). Rare white glazed porcelain shoulder head boy doll. The lower legs are of turned wood, the arms are white bisque and his body is hand-sewn cloth. (Private Collection)

'Frozen Charlotte'

1850~1860

Fig 5a. 2in (5cm). 'Frozen Charlotte', made of pink tinted glazed porcelain a doll without any articulation whatever. (Author's Collection)

Fig 5b

Fig 5a,b is a 2in (5cm) pink tinted glazed porcelain doll without any articulation whatever. This type is variously known as a Pudding Doll, Bathing Doll, Pillar Doll and Frozen Charlotte — the latter being its currently most popular description. This rigid doll ranged in sizes from over two feet in height to less than an inch and the tiniest were reputedly cooked in the Christmas pudding.

This specimen has a white moulded bonnet with ribbon ties painted in red and like most Frozen Charlottes depicts a toddler. Her features are painted with the utmost simplicity: black dots for eyes, black eyelines, single stroke black eyebrows and dark vermillion lips with two dots for nostrils. The blushmarks on the cheeks are subtle for the type, particularly in this small size. The pink complexion coat however is uneven and patchy. Sleek black centre-parted hair is painted on the forehead to show below the bonnet. There is minimal modelling in the hands and bare feet though the body is well shaped. The rigid arms are bent at the elbows and terminate in small cupped downturned hands.

The doll's dress is made of two strips of scarlet satin ribbon and a band of lace. The ribbon used for the top of the dress is gathered at the shoulders with holes allowing the arms through. The lower ribbon and lace are gathered at the waist. The method of dressmaking used is extremely simple but the result undeniably effective. The doll's silhouette is typically that of a toddler of the mid-nineteenth century.

1850-1860

Seated 'Frozen Charlotte'

Fig 6. 1¼in (3cm). Seated 'Frozen Charlotte' of untinted glazed porcelain. This example was found in a walnut shell. (Author's Collection)

Fig 6. Charlottes also came "frozen" in a seated position though these are more rare than the standing type. The 1¼in (3cm) example shown here was found contained in a walnut shell that had metal hinges and a catch and silk ribbons by which it may have been intended to be suspended from a Christmas tree. Many miniature toys of wood, ivory and porcelain are found in walnut cases, and as the walnut harvest is the period immediately preceding Christmas it seems logical to assume that these artifacts were manufactured for the seasonal toy trade.

This doll is one of the best of the tinies and her face has a sweet expression with upwards sideways glancing eyes adding great appeal to a diminutive specimen which in this scale is more usually gimcrack and devoid of character.

She is of untinted glazed porcelain with black painted hair and clear comb marks in her short infant hairstyle. The eyes, eyelines and brows are black with scarlet lips and nose dots and softly rouged cheeks. Her bent limbs are beautifully modelled and tiny fists have clear fingers and thumbs. The dress is a scrap of rose coloured silk minutely gathered at the shoulders and caught at the waist with cotton strands. This commercially made garment has its hem gathered, closed and padded to facilitate a firm seat within the original nutshell container.

Seated 'Frozen Charlie'

1850-1860

Fig 7. 2in (5cm). Seated 'Frozen Charlie', photographed seated at a piano showing how readily such dolls found acceptance within the dolls' house. (Courtesy Jill Lewis)

Fig 7. Another example of a seated Frozen Charlotte is this 2in (5cm) specimen with a hairstyle clearly intended to represent a boy. Among Bathing Dolls alone the number of girls and boys seems to be about equal and the charming term of Frozen Charlie has been coined for the male version.

Of untinted glazed porcelain, the doll has a smooth ball head leaving the indication of the hair entirely to the brush of the decorator. The style is windswept and side parted with fine brush strokes all around the face. The hair colour is the usual black as are the eyes, eyelines and brows. Smiling lips and nose dots are scarlet and rather patchy blush marks give colour to the cheeks. The modelling of the body and limbs is vague and the hands are little more than paws. The feet however do have an indication of toes.

His homemade dress is a piece of pink ribbon gathered at the shoulders and waist. He is photographed seated at a piano to show how readily such dolls found acceptance within the dolls' house.

Opinions vary on maximum heights at which a doll ceases to qualify as a dolls' house type and falls into the category of playdoll. Surprisingly there are few queries at the diminutive end of this scale where the purpose of some 'tinies' was patently ambiguous. Perhaps the lesson to be taken from this is that any doll found in a dolls' house can be categorised as a resident provided the respective scales of doll and house are in unison. Some houses were extremely small while others were of mammoth proportions, but these are rare extremes and their contents once disseminated are not always recognised for their true purpose. The issue remains debatable, but collectors generally have settled for 9in (23cm) as the maximum height for dolls' house dolls.

1850-1860 # Girl with bonnet

Fig 8 stands precisely 9in including her intricately moulded bonnet and is in every way a most distinguished doll. The oval face with finely chiselled features is artistically framed by moulded trim of leaves and flowers and ruffles on either side of the cheeks. To round off the well balanced encircling decoration a pink ribbon tie is painted below the chin. The yellow bonnet is modelled in excellent detail with a pink lustre feather across the back of the brim. The bisque shoulder head is delicately painted in bland tones. Blue eyes have dark ochre eyelines, red lid lines and eye and nose dots and also lips of palest rose. Hair and eyebrows are light ochre.

The doll has long bisque lower arms with much detail in the hands and bisque legs with narrow black boots. Her hand-sewn red wool dress is liberally lace trimmed, partially lined and is a home product of inferior merit. The mid-calf drawers and petticoat are commercially made of starched fine gauze. The shapely cloth body is white and the figure in outline suggests a girl of the late 1850's

Fig 8. 9in (23cm). A most distinguished bisque shoulder head, with long bisque lower arms and bisque legs with narrow black boots. The shapely cloth body is white and the figure in outline suggests a girl of the late 1850's. (Courtesy Moira Garland)

1860~1870

1860-1870   'Timeless Beauty'

Fig 9a,b,c,d. Everything about this doll has been conceived with skill and subtlety. The face has a timeless beauty admirably balanced between delicacy and bold splendour. Here surely is the perfect portrayal of the flower of Victorian "indoor plants" untainted by wind and weather, yet with an undeniable air of sophistication. This dolls' waterfall coiffeur of the early 60's is a pure yellow ochre with the centre parting continuing down the back of the head. The sides are puffed and the back hair is arranged in a cadogan. In life this hairstyle involved the addition of false pieces. At the centre top of her head is a remaining piece of an applied ultramarine ornament and hanging from this half vanished anchorage is a moulded gold lustre jewel resting on the forehead. At both temples there are painted ribbon bows in ultramarine specked with violet and with moulded clasps. The dolls' pendant earrings are also gold lustre as is the decorative comb supporting the cadogan at the back.

Fig 9a. 6in (15cm). A bisque shoulder head doll of superlative quality. The shoulders slope steeply from the neck and are very deep — the shoulder head itself accounting for one third of the doll's height. The bisque is very high grade. The doll's arms are long and well shaped with two creases at the wrist and well defined fingers and thumbs. (Author's Collection)

Fig 9b

16

'Timeless Beauty' 1860~1870

Fig 9c

The features are painted with notable merit. Eyes are Prussian blue with the iris placed directly beneath the black eyelines and there are red lid-lines. The finely arched brows are painted dark ochre. Red dots at eye corners and nostrils. The shoulders slope steeply from the neck and are very deep — the shoulder head itself accounting for one third of the dolls' height which is 6in (15cm). The bisque is very high grade. The doll's arms are long and well shaped with two creases at the wrist and well defined fingers and thumbs. Her legs wear moulded black ankle boots without heels and with light brown soles.

Her high-necked black dress marks the closing days of the crinolines' reign. The hemline is still a perfect circle, but the long favoured pointed bodice has given way to a rounded waist. The two-tiered skirt is decorated with a rouched chiffon round its central perimeter. The upper tier has a scalloped hemline, the lower is of box pleated satin. Where the diaphanous corsage meets the bodice there is an encircling rouched chiffon ribbon and the long sleeves are also chiffon. The coral velvet tie at the waist provides a single touch of colour to a sombre dress executed with panache.

Fig 9d

1860-1870   Small boy doll

Fig 10. 3½in (9cm). Boy doll dressed in the manner of the mid-1860's. His body is of pink cloth and his shoulder head and lower arms are of lightly tinted bisque (Private Collection)

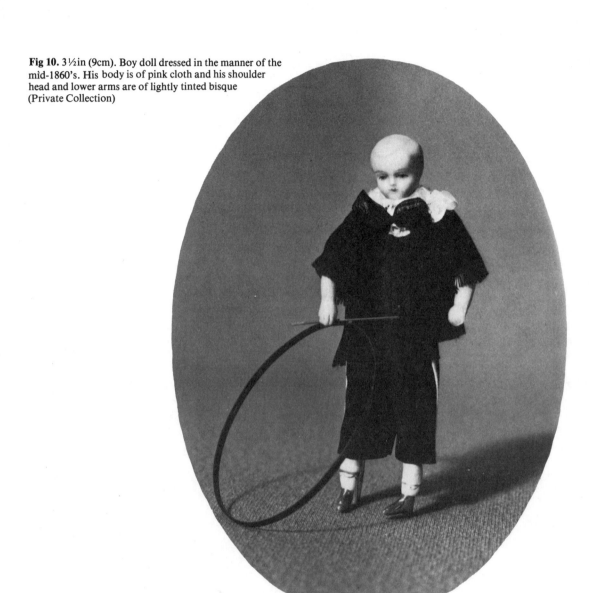

Fig 10. The vogue for physical inactivity was not confined to women alone. Children were equally affected by this langourous behaviour and outgoing activities were discouraged. It is therefore not surprising that this small boy doll shares the delicate palor currently so admired and delicately nurtured by the opposite sex.

3½in (9cm) high, he is dressed in the manner of the mid-1860's in black silk taffeta with calf-length trousers and matching tunic tied at the waist with a black sash. His deep collar is of cream chiffon and the bow at his neck of black chiffon. Cream is repeated in the fine braiding on the outer leg of the trousers.

His body is pink cloth and his shoulder head and lower arms are of lightly tinted bisque. His lower legs present the most outstanding feature of the doll. From the knees down to mid calf the bisque is tinted but from here down the legs are glazed and represent white socks decorated with painted pink looped ribbons. Ankle length boots have heels and are gold lustre. Soles of the boots are pearl lustre.

The dolls' stance with inward turning toes is delightfully deferential. Blonde hair is side-parted with very little modelling and without comb marks. The facial decoration is of high quality with scarlet lips and nose dots, blue eyes, black eyelines and brows to match the hair. This doll was found together with the lady doll in the previous illustration. (Fig 9.)

Small boy in tunic

1860-1870

Fig 11. 3½in (9cm). This doll depicts a small boy of the mid-nineteenth century, he is of good quality bisque with a light brown cloth body. (Private Collection)

Fig 11 depicts a 3½in (9cm) small boy in a red and black belted tunic with white drawers showing below the hem. This fashion was general for male children under five years of age, attaining the height of popularity during the middle of the nineteenth century. It seems probable that this carefully made outfit is a miniature replica, as so much scale and effect has been sacrificed to its detailed construction. The doll appears positively swaddled in his party dress.

He is of good quality bisque with fine modelling in the head and limbs. The body is light brown cloth. His moulded light ochre side-parted hair is waved all over and the ears are exposed. The hands are small with fingers and thumbs clearly represented. The narrow feet wear pointed grey/black ankle boots with brick coloured soles. The eyes are light blue with dark ochre eyelines and light ochre brows; the lips and nose dots are pale orange. All features are carefully painted though the right eye is off-centre adding the comical touch of a squint to the little trussed-up specimen.

The tunic is made of two panels of different materials. The front section is red silk shirred vertically and stitched at its centre and side edges with black thread. The back and long sleeves are black velvet and the whole is tied with a red ribbon sash. A small lace collar is threaded with red silk and ties at the back of the neck. Underwear comprises a white cotton petticoat, another of red flannel and cotton drawers edged with tatting.

1860-1870

Fashionable Lady

The period from 1860 to the mid-70's was the dazzling heyday of the dressmakers' art. Every conceivable intricacy of detail and complication of design was contrived for displaying her expertise. The essential message of feminine dress was directly related to the wealth and position of the wearer. The Victorian gentleman however remained judiciously clad in colourless unchanging sobriety. It was left to the wife and daughters of his household to advertise his status and add kudos to his rank by adorning themselves with unashamed opulence — the degree of finery being the highest expression of the providers' riches. This intricate exercise in display provided a two-fold advantage. It kept at a distance those beneath one's social station thus avoiding any regretable infringements in a society which was much concerned with everyone knowing their place. To the increasing string of newcomers to every strata the significance was by no means lost and the shadow of this practice is cast far down into our own time. The extravagancies of Victorian fashions are today superceded by the modified symbols of furs and jewels, but the message is still the same. The feminine practice of displaying the degree of success enjoyed by her husband continues to perform the age old function of at once indicating personal wealth and forming an obtrusive bastion to keep others at bay.

Fig 12a,b provides an intimate picture through her mode of dress of the charmed circle she inhabits. The unbridled enthusiasm for decoration has produced an overloaded

Fig 12a. 5in (13cm). The lower limbs are of turned wood, gessoed and painted. The body is of hand sewn brown linen and the white bisque shoulder head is conspicuous both in its modelling and its sure-handed brushwork. (Private Collection)

Fashionable Lady

1860-1870

affect. A single glance at the ball gown she wears is sufficient to assure one that in full scale it would have necessitated the employment of many seamstresses at some considerable cost. Every outward and visible sign has been lavished upon the miniature image of this lady displaying her rank and fortune by her dress and its embellishments as surely as a string of signals flying from a ship's mast.

The height of the doll is 5in (13cm) and her lower limbs are of turned wood, gessoed and painted. The hands are the spade type with thumbs free standing. The black ankle boots are sharply pointed, flat and with a yellow base. The body is of hand sewn brown linen. The white bisque shoulder head is conspicuous both in its modelling and its sure handed brushwork.

The style of dress and evening coiffeur suggests the date 1863 but some of the materials from which the crinoline dress is made establish that the doll was re-dressed in the twentieth century. The unity of hair and dress styles points to a possibility of a replica. The arrangement of the moulded hair is intricate on a matt light ochre ground with finely etched comb marks. In life this style involved the division of the hair into three equal masses: The central portion waved and puffed in front, continuing down the back and terminating in a cadogan at the nape of the neck. The two side portions, puffed at the temples were drawn into braids eclipsing the ears, passing across the cadogan and fastening beneath it.

The dolls' distinctive face has light blue eyes, black eyelines, dark ochre brows, rose coloured lips and nose dots. The cheeks are faintly rouged. The doll is a most artistic product, the more remarkable when one takes into account that its original purpose was one of nursery trivia.

Fig 12b

21

1860-1870   Fashion doll

Fig 13. 5½in (14cm). This untinted bisque shoulder-head doll is in every detail a classic example of a fashionable woman of the mid-1860's. (Author's Collection)

Fig 13. The 5½in (14cm) doll shown here is in every detail a classic example of a fashionable woman of the mid-1860's. From the top of her moulded evening coiffeur to the tip of her flat heeled ankle boots she epitomises all that was considered desirable to the contemporary concept of beauty. A white complexion was considered essential to feminine good looks in an age when faces were vigilantly shielded from fresh air and sunlight.

The doll's lilac and cream dress and its trimmings follow the vogue of 1865 to the letter, when the crinoline skirt was double and in two colours with the fullness of the upper skirt drawn to the back — the first sign of the bustle which was to be established by the 70's. Tiers of pleats form the main decoration of the skirt and floral sprays, lace and bows adorn the dress. The low decolletage and pointed bodice are evidence that the doll is dressed for an evening occasion. The sleeves are pagoda style not quite reaching the wrists. The moulded coiffeur is a glossy dark brown and has well defined comb marks with brushstrokes at the temples. The ears are partially covered and two long ringlets fall on either side of the face to the front of the shoulders. The back hair is arranged in corkscrew curls. The star-shaped sequins glued to the hair and further evidence of this being a style for evening wear. This was a period when small brilliant jewels adorned elaborately dressed hair, taking precidence over flower and feather decoration. The pendant necklace is incredibly applied gold paper.

It must be confessed that this elegant doll dressed for a formal occasion owns not a vestige of underwear! Her body and upper limbs are of dark brown hand sewn linen. Her shoulder head and lower limbs are of untinted bisque. Features are well painted with eyes and eyebrows matching the hair colour. The cheeks are rouged and her decorator has left the simulacrum of a thumb print to posterity on one cheek! Lips are a soft red. Her pointed boots are painted black with soles of light yellow.

Pageboy in livery

1860-1870

Fig 14. A cursory glance might lead one to suppose that this 5½in (14cm) male doll is dressed in the manner of a cavalier of the early 1800's. Certainly much in his appearance points to a dress suit of this period. His frac, lace jabot, silver embroidered waistcoat and knee breeches would be typical, as are his flat heeled black pointed shoes and white stockinged legs. His short waved and curled hair and clean shaven face are very much in keeping. Dolls were not infrequently dressed in representation of earlier modes and the dolls' house variety found ready acceptance as marionettes in that popular toy the miniature theatre. The writer has seen a collection of "actors" with metal rods sewn to their cloth bodies beneath their fancy dress.

However this doll is certainly not of such an early period. He is the companion of Fig 13 and his stylish outfit shares some of the materials used in her dress. We must therefore conclude that this seemingly dandified gentleman is in fact a personal attendant — a pageboy in livery!

His shoulder head and lower arms are of bisque delicately tinted to give an unusual lightly tanned appearance. His lower legs are of white glazed porcelain and the painted black shoes have light brown soles. He has blue eyes with brown eyelines and brows. There are eye and nostril dots. The smiling mouth is vermillion and there are faint blush marks on the cheeks. The dark brown hair has a side parting with brush strokes at the temples. His ears are well modelled and quite protruding but his small hands lack definition. Body and upper limbs are beige hand sewn cloth.

His frac of lilac silk is trimmed with fuschia braiding and the collar is edged with silver. His silk waistcoat is violet and excessively decorated with silver thread embroidery and sequins. Ivory silk breeches have a single sequin on the outer side of each leg and a fuschia tassel.

Fig 14. 5½in (14cm). This male doll is the companion to the lady shown in Fig 13. His shoulder head and lower arms are of bisque delicately tinted to give an unusual tanned appearance. (Author's Collection)

1860-1870　　　　　　　　　Wedding Group

Fig 15. Group depicting a marriage scene. (Author's Collection)

Fig 15. The virtuosity of dolls' house dolls is illustrated here in a group depicting a marriage scene. Such specimens recording an event were usually dressed in the home and are frequently found in mint order as these mementos were often housed beneath glass shades. It was customary for the cuttings of the materials worn by the people represented to be used on the dolls, and these nostalgic keepsakes can reflect accurately the textiles of their time. This is rarely true of other home dressed dolls where the materials may be several decades earlier.

Bride doll

1860-1870

Fig 15a. 4¼in (11cm). A beautiful bride with the moulded hairstyle popular throughout the 1860's. The doll's facial decoration is a triumph of miniature brushwork. (Author's Collection)

Fig 15a. The striking 4¼in (11cm) bride has an oval face and slender neck with a moulded hairstyle that was a firm favourite throughout the 1860's. This is surprisingly well defined on such a diminished scale. Centre parted and waved, the hair is drawn back into a moulded ribbon caul encasing the entire coiffeur. Small ribbon bowknots are moulded on either side of the face and the whole is in the light blonde colouring of the hair. The doll's facial decoration is a triumph of miniature brushwork. The eyes are cobalt blue with black eyelines and red lid lines. Lips and nose dots are a soft red and the eyebrows light ochre. Cheeks are lightly rouged. The face very aptly wears a dreamy expression caused by the upper and lower perimeters of the iris being obscured by the lid lines.

Bridal gowns are not notably reflective of contemporary styles and to this day classical modes are still favoured to ensure against rapid dating. Nevertheless prevailing fashions influence all garments and from a mélé of styles one can arrive at a probable date from the latest aspects of the gown.

The wedding dress is of cream silk taffeta self trimmed at the hem and lace trimmed at the low decolletage. The lace upper skirt is drawn to the back extending far behind the under skirt. The luxurious veil and oversleeves are of gossamer chiffon with lace edging and a coronet of silver 'fan lace' rests on the centre top of the head where it has been glued, securing two pendant streamers of cream fan lace. Ribbon bowknots decorate the shoulders and hem flounce and a ribbon encircles the waist drawn through a steel buckle. The neckline, belted waist and lace streamers are features of the previous decade, but the general silhouette reflects a date in the mid-1860's. The bridal bouquet is of flowers in coloured glass and miniscule white sea shells wired together and tied with looped silk ribbons. The dolls' bisque shoulder head is deep and sloping and her lower limbs of bisque are slender and elongated. Legs wear black boots with pointed toes and yellow soles.

1860-1870

Bridegroom and Bridesmaids

Fig 15b. 4¾in (12cm). The bridegroom. He has a bisque shoulder head with crisply defined features. (Author's Collection)

Fig 15b. The 4¾in (12cm) bridegroom has a bisque shoulder head with crisply defined features and good brushwork decoration. The moulded blond side-parted hair has comb marks and the ears are well modelled. The blue painted eyes are large and black eyelines are not in the usual unbroken line but suggest eyelashes. Lips and nose dots are a soft red with light ochre eyebrows and rosy cheeks.

His clothes comprise a shirt of microscopic vertical tucks with a lace jabot and a tiepin represented by a star-shaped sequin. His suit is black serge and the tailcoat with deep lapels is decorated with a floral buttonhole of ribbon rosettes. Silver beads serve as two buttons and the doll wears a black velvet cummerbund. Cuffs of lace are visible at the wrists and a black felt hat is glued to the right hand.

It is not possible to inspect this dolls' body as he is securely sewn into his clothes, but arms are seen to be white bisque and legs of white glazed porcelain with grape lustre boots.

Fig 15c. This somewhat comical trio representing the bridesmaids are all-bisque dolls articulated at the shoulders and hips and standing approximately 2in (5cm) in height. They have moulded short curled hair of dark ochre with central partings and comb marks. Their rather haphazardly painted features gives each a quite individual expression added to which differing minor details disclose that they did not share the same mould design. They are however dressed in identical outfits. Their lace dresses are trimmed and almost entirely swamped by two rows of shirred ribbon; the lower of pink silk, the upper of ivory chiffon. This chiffon is repeated at the bodice and its bulk serves to cover the arms in a semblence of sleeves. Each has a petticoat of linen embroidered at the hem in red. Shoes are moulded and painted black. All three have a posy looped round the wrist of wired sea shells and glued to the tops of their heads are what appear to be the remains of sized net caps from which pink and white ribbon streamers hang in the back.

Fig 15c. 2in (5cm). The bridesmaids are all-bisque dolls articulated at the shoulders and hips. (Author's Collection)

Priest

1860-1870

Fig 15d. 4¼in (11cm). The priest. His bisque shoulder head and lower limbs are rather powdery in texture. (Author's Collection)

Fig 15d is the priest of the wedding group and is 4¼in (11cm) high. His bisque shoulder head and lower limbs are rather powdery in texture and lack-lustre in tone. The decorators paint also has a faded appearance and it seems possible that these muted tones influenced the choice of this doll for his role. Beside the delicately tinted bride and groom and the positively robust complexions of the bridesmaids, he recedes into sombre sobriety effectively concealing that the doll in fact represents a young boy!

His sandy hair is moulded from a centre crown without any parting in a forward swept style emphasised by comb marks and brush strokes. Eyes are blue with black eyelines, brown eye brows and nose dots and lips in soft red. He has no blush marks on the cheeks. The ears are large and well modelled. Fingers are nebulous. Legs wear black moulded boots with yellow soles. Body is beige cloth. His cassock and cape are of black felt, the cape having some remains of a white silk edging. The surplice made of cotton is minutely pleated and can be seen from the protected areas to have once been white.

1860-1870 # Fashion doll

Fig 16a,b is a 4½in (12cm) doll displaying a hairdo which dates her mould to circa 1850 and her dress to some fifteen years later. During the 50's no specific hairstyle reigned supreme. Women were encouraged to choose from the variations in fashion that which best suited their personal characteristics. Whichever of the many complex styles was selected from the melange of ringlets, buns, knots, loops, braids and chignons, it was essential for day wear that the style should be modifed and worn without decoration. It was also necessary for the top hair to be sleek in order to accommodate that indispensable outdoor accessory — the bonnet.

The centre parted moulded coiffeur of this doll represents in a somewhat stylised form a tightly packed row of vertical sausage curls giving fullness to the sides of the face with a severely flattened top ready for the all important headgear. The style is associated with young women and little girls, suggesting that although these dolls have the appearance of ladies they may well have been manufactured in representation of children. This simple symmetrical moulded coiffeur is found in greater proliferation among dolls' house dolls than any other style.

Fig 16b

Fig 16a. 4½in (12cm). The bisque shoulder head and limbs are white and of the type known as 'greasey' bisque. An unusual feature are chestnut brown heel-less ankle boots. (Private Collection)

The mode of the doll's crinoline day dress has the fullness of the skirt receding towards the back which was a feature of 1865. The waist has a belt of self material decorated at the front and back with circles of silver beads. There are also silver beads sewn vertically to the front in representation of a buttoned bodice. The front panel of the skirt is flounced at the hem and on either side from the waist to the base of the panel. The back of the skirt is cut in three sections and has two tiers of flouncing. The elbow length sleeves of the pagoda type are again typical of the mid-60's. The dress is entirely of green silk taffeta, the only colour variation being provided by a yellow rouched ribbon at the high neckline. The skirt was lined with paper for support of which now only fragments remain.

The doll's hair is café-au-lait with matching eyebrows. Her blue eyes are unusual in that they have no pupils but in their place are white highlight dots. Eyelines are black and the lips a dark orange. The bisque shoulder head and lower limbs are white and of the type known as "greasey" bisque. Cloth body is peach coloured and an unusual feature are chestnut brown heel-less ankle boots.

Hatted doll

1860-1870

Fig 17 is a Hatted Doll of the late 1860's with all her aspects in perfect harmony. From her forward tilting hat to the braided hem of her pyramidal skirt she is the complete embodiment of high fashion in the closing years of that decade. The transitional period between the crinoline and the bustle was the pannier dress, also known as the tunic dress when the bodice was attached to, and of the same material as, the panniered overskirt. This style was not worn over a hooped cage as the wide hipped look was achieved by the panniers, and was the prelude of the bustle, ante-dating it by a mere two years when the fetish for exaggerated fullness somewhere on the skirt began slipping from the sides towards the back.

5½in (14cm) from the top of her moulded hat to her flat heeled ankle boots, the doll's lovely features exact a crispness from the untinted bisque, her facial characteristics reflecting the idealised adaptation of realism to the requirements of contemporary taste. The flat crowned hat is painted yellow with a black band. A pink moulded rose rests on the narrow brim in front and a grape lustre plume entirely covers the right half of the hat, descending in a curve and resting on the dark brown coiffeur. The style is puffed round exposed ears and arranged in vertical curls worn low on the neck. Delicate painting enhances the clarity of her features — dark blue eyes, black eyelines, dark brown eyebrows and rose coloured narrow lips. There are light blushmarks on the cheeks of this otherwise "white-skinned" lady doll. Her deep sloping bare shoulders add a measure of femininity to a specimen delightfully tinged with the graceful spirit of her ambience.

The wide gored underskirt is of cream silk grosgrain embroidered with a rose motif, each wedge-shaped section being delineated by gold braid which also embellishes the huge base circumference. The bodice and overskirt of rose silk grosgrain are richly scattered with matching ribbon, artificial flowers, dried fern and gold beads. These have been applied to every available area on the front of the dress in such proliferation that they have become entirely intermixed. No less than ten ribbon rosettes comprising streamers, ferns, flowers and beads decorate the corsage, panniers and sleeves. In addition, a spray of ferns and flowers are clustered into a posy tied to the doll's right wrist. The narrow sleeves repeat the material of the underskirt but have gold embroidery at their deep rouched cuffs which start at the elbows and terminate above the wrists. The pyramid shaped underskirt is lined with muslin and achieves its distension from two wide buckram petticoats. Drawers reaching below the knees are also of buckram. The doll's lower limbs of untinted bisque are fashioned with good detail. Her small hands have defined fingers and thumbs and the tiny black boots are painted on delicately rounded legs decorated at their top with pink ribbon garters.

Fig 17. 5½in (14cm). Hatted doll of the late 1860's. She has a moulded hat and flat-heeled ankle boots. (Courtesy Moira Garland)

This flamboyant gorgeously coloured hand made outfit with its confusion of embellishments, the flashy little moulded hat, the doll's delicate palor and neatly contained coiffeur blend together in such harmonious detail, that one can say without doubt that she was manufactured and dressed in the year 1868.

1860-1870   'Haute-monde' doll

Fig 18a. 5½in (14cm). This doll wears a style which is associated with the closing years of the 60's and which one also recognises as being of 'haute monde'. (Author's Collection)

Fig 18b

Fig 18a,b. The Victorian era is to many synonymous with prudery. Vulgarity was supposedly intolerable with refinement and restraint the prescribed form. In spite of idealised concepts of modest propriety, female dress was remarkably provocative and evening wear for women was often a veritable arsenal of inuendos. As the all-concealing crinoline gave way to the bustle of the 70's, womens' clothes took on a surpassing grace with the emphasis on natural feminine curves resulting in flowing lines and an extravagant use of materials. The length of dress and the amount of material used held great significance.

This doll wears a style which is associated with the closing years of the 60's and which one also recognises as being of the haute monde. A skirt of such trailing length and volume speaks of rooms on a grandiose scale. Surely this striking creature is an aristocrat at the very least — dressed for a formal afternoon occasion. Her two-toned dress of honey coloured satin and dove gray figured grosgrain is trimmed with fine écru lace. It is lined throughout with muslin and beneath it the doll wears a voluminous pleated buckram petticoat. The elevated coiffeur is in perfect keeping with the doll's dress. During the late 60's, day wear hair fashions rose in the back and this resulted in a delightful vogue for small forward tilting hats often with long "flirtation streamers" which tied behind beneath the upswept chignon flowing back and creating a perfect balance between the head and trained skirt. These ribbons were also termed "follow-me-lads" which strikes a contradictory note in an age when to do just that would have been unthinkable.

Coquetry is not generally associated with Victorian mannerisms but fashions from the time often prove this to be a mistaken idea. To emphasise this point, this doll has a finely sculptured bosom with a clearly stated cleavage which her square-necked dress (very fashionable at this time) shows off to the greatest possible advantage. Her shepherdess hat is of simulated straw and appears to be moulded plaster mounted on a silk base. It is yellow with white ribbon ties and is decorated with a single feather. Her hair is most elaborately arranged. Painted a light blond matt colour, it has a moulded band in the centre front the same colour as the hair itself but picked out by an application of glaze. The front hair is waved with a centre parting and the sides puffed out and drawn upwards to tuck over the band. The back hair is upswept into a chignon. Her bisque is untinted with faint rouging on the cheeks. The eyes are ultramarine with well modelled upper and lower lids. Eyebrows are dark ochre and the lips and nose dots scarlet. The ears are well defined and are pierced for earrings. The lower arms of white bisque have been wrongly assembled — the right being in the place of the left and vice versa. The hands are very small and flat. The lower legs also of white bisque have black boots painted on with black flat soles. The doll stands 5½in (14cm) high and her body is of beige cloth. This model comes in varying sizes, some as high as 25in (64cm).

1870~1880

1870-1880　　　　　　　　　　　Lady doll

Fig 19a,b is a 5½in (14cm) lady doll with a shoulder head of white glazed porcelain with black moulded hair arranged in a style associated with the mid-nineteenth century. Her dress however dates to the 1870's and one concludes that she was re-dressed by a second generation because her cloth body is of the early brown hand-sewn type. Also the manner of fixing the shoulder-head to the torso through sew holes front and back (Fig 19b) precedes the later method of glueing. Her sleek centre parted coiffeur with exaggerated side puffs eclipsing the ears and the coiled bun at the back is classical of fashionable styling for the early 50's. The hair is painted black without brush strokes or comb marks. The doll has light blue painted eyes with black eyelines and brows. The lips are pale orange and there are light blushmarks on the white complexion ground. The glazed lower arms are fashioned as fists and the lower legs of white bisque have painted black ankle boots.

Fig 19a. 5½in (14cm). Lady doll with a shoulder head of white glazed porcelain with black moulded hair. (Author's Collection)

Lady doll

1870-1880

The doll's evening dress is made of two contrasting materials. The bodice with a low square cut yoke is of blue embroidered silk which continues down the back forming a large bustle. The skirt of cream satin is adorned most lavishly with lace, sequins, beads and embroidered flowers. The sleeves share an equal proportion of both materials. A rosette of lilac ribbon is pinned through the front sew hole at once disguising its presence and serving to embellish the low decolletage. Beneath her trained dress the doll wears a petticoat of net and another of linen. A charming touch is the "choker" round her throat made of black thread and a single gold sequin effectively suggesting a locket suspended from a velvet ribbon.

Fig 19b

1870-1880 — Lady doll with fan

Fig 20a,b is 6¾in (17cm) high without complexion tinting and with very considerable detail of modelling. Her moulded coiffeur is particularly prodigeous in comb marks. The style suggests that the mould from which this head was cast was manufactured not earlier than 1863. The front hair is brushed off the face and the sides are rolled forwards over a black band in a succession of rolls and waves which continue vertically round the back of the head, the crown remaining smooth. The half exposed ears are pierced and wear small pearl earrings. Her clearly sculptured features and sensitive decoration result in a little doll of noble presence. Her hair colour is dark blond with matching eyebrows. Blue eyes are painted beneath moulded eyelids and light vermillion lips follow the small sculptured mouth accurately.

The features of her dress have been executed with very considerable talent from a piece of oriental embroidered silk of vibrant kingfisher blue and olive green. It is trimmed with lace, dark blue ribbon and artificial flowers and fruit. The cuirasse bodice is decorated with a plastron of ribbon strips. The pagoda sleeves and crinoline skirt (flattened in front but not yet tied back into the tubular shape a few years ahead), the trained back and bustle all blend to establish the vogue

Fig 20a. 6¾in (17cm). The clearly sculptured features and sensitive decoration make this a little doll of noble presence. (Private Collection)

of the early 70's. Only the silk berthe collar transcends the frontiers of time, being an evening dress feature of the period between 1850 and 60. Whether this desultory feature was an airy concoction on the part of the seamstress, or whether it was a force of circumstance — one meagre strip remaining to fill an area of yoke as best could be, one can only guess at. Such features impairing unity of style are found with surprising frequency and one explanation may be that the dressmaking was undertaken by members of the older generation and that these ladies indulged in a little nostalgia, still favouring the fashions of their own youth. The large fan 'held' by the doll matches the lace of her collar and undersleeves, and her necklace of glass beads repeats the green of her gown. The dolls' body is peach coloured cloth and her white bisque legs have painted black ankle boots. The lower arms have a common fault of wrong assembly — both being right arms.

Fig 20b

Lady with parasol 1870-1880

Fig 21. 5½in (14cm). Originally from the same miniature interior as Fig 20 this doll has clearly been dressed by the same hand. (Author's Collection)

Fig 21. Originally from the same miniature interior as Fig 20 comes this 5½in (14cm) doll clearly dressed by the same hand and sharing with her companion not only the lace trim but all the dislocated recollections of fashion features spanning two decades. Because fashion can never see ahead, one must estimate the doll's date by her latest aspect — in this instance the hairstyle. During the 1880's fashionable feminine coiffeur was worn in inflated styles with abundant false additions usually directed upwards and to the back in waves, puffs and rolls. Crimping and frizzing became all the rage during this decade which saw the birth of the Marcel Wave.

The doll's light ochre moulded hairdo is of the vogue from the early 80's and is decorated with blue and gold glazed ribbon bands showing at the temples and on top in front as a bow. The exposed ears wear large moulded glazed earrings. Her shoulder head and lower limbs are of white bisque with good modelling. The decoration is bright and distinct — blue eyes with dark ochre eyelines, red lid lines and dark ochre eyebrows. Smiling vermillion lips, nostril dots and rouged cheeks all demonstrate a high standard of brushwork.

The dress is composed essentially of features dating to the 1870's with its flattened skirt front, low bustle and trained back, but once again this seamstresses treatment in introducing a deep lace berthe gives an account of her disregard for stylistic accuracy. Clearly her imagination was led effortlessly back down the years resulting in a doll of the 80's wearing a dress of the 70's with a collar of the 60's! The evening dress is made from a broad band of ice blue figured and embroidered silk grosgrain. The front section of the skirt is piped on either side with yellow silk which has also been used to trim the base of the skirt and for two rosettes on the hips. The bustle is decorated at its base with a cluster of yellow paper flowers and a blue tassel. The narrow three-quarter-length sleeves are trimmed at the cuffs with lace and decorated at the shoulders with pink ribbon bowknots.

The doll has a beige cloth body and her underwear consists of two linen petticoats and matching mid-calf drawers. The legs have painted grey/black flat heeled ankle boots. Faulty assembly has endowed the doll with two left arms. Her contemporary parasol is ivory and the fan enamelled silver.

1870-1880   # Peg-jointed doll

Fig 22. 3¼in (8cm). Beautifully painted eyes are an outstanding feature of this bisque headed doll with all wood torso and limbs.
(Author's Collection)

Fig 22 is 3¼in (8cm) high with an all-wood torso and limbs and a pink tinted bisque shoulder head. This is secured to the body by a wooden dowel passing up inside the head where it is fixed with glue. There is little or no modelling to the head itself; the most prominent feature being the raised join marks left by the casting moulds which is usually better sanded off before decoration. Ears are totally absent and all other features are barely in relief, but the decorators brush has done much to add merit to this most individual specimen and the colouring is subtle and efficiently applied. The equivocal nature of the café-au-lait coloured hair will have made the doll freely adaptable to a male or a female dolls' house child. Its beautifully painted eyes are large and dark blue with big pupils and black eyelines. The single stroke brows are dark ochre and lips and nose dots a pale rose so light in tone as to be scarcely discernable. The cheeks are lightly rouged and blend well into the complexion coat.

The body is peg-jointed at the shoulders, elbows, hips and knees. The upper and lower sections of the arms are painted pink with very small simply carved hands with mere notches for thumbs. The lower legs have white painted stockings and flat heeled light grey ankle boots on diminutive feet. There is no gessoe or varnish and the matt paintwork appears to be water colour.

1880~1890

1880-1890

Horatia Jones family group

Fig 23

Fig. 23 The following five dolls are of particular interest as they are of that rare species — the fully documented doll! They were the childhood toys of Horatia Jones and were dressed for her by her aunt Tamzine Billing in 1886. Labels in "Aunt Tammy's" handwriting are sewn to their clothes identifying the person that each doll represents. The dolls are part of a vast cache found in Horatia's cabinet-dolls'-house after her death in 1969

Though consistency of scale within the dolls' house sphere is known to have been of little consequence, it is in this instance significant that the height of the dolls chosen for each individual seemingly held some implication for the adult who dressed them.

The Victorian father was unquestionably the head of his household, and this fact could hardly be more patently stated than by allowing the doll that represents him an additional height of two inches over the ladies of the group. The fact that his head is quite out of proportion to that of the women was seemingly of little account and apparently infinitely preferable to a lack of emphasis of his elevated position in the family hierarchy.

It is also telling that the child Horatia is represented by a minute doll which beside "Papa" assumes the proportions of a figurine! Even to her mother's scale she would present a mere toddler and as it is known that the dolls were dressed for her when she was ten years old, the inference must be the prevalent attitude towards children. While the Victorian child was regarded with sentiment, it nevertheless exercised little significance as an individual within the home beyond that of being seen and not heard, and what better way to give expression to this concept than by choosing the smallest doll available for the portrayal of the child. What a revealing testimony these dolls provide of the great attention paid to personal status — even within the confines of the family structure.

Sir Horace Jones

1880-1890

Fig 24. The 8½in (22cm) doll has been cunningly transformed to maturity by the application of a flocked grey beard, side whiskers and moustaches glued to his face and around the back of the head. He is labelled "My Dada at Breakfast" and represents Sir Horace Jones — Horatia's father. The doll's deep shoulder head is of high grade untinted bisque of the type known as "greasey". The lower limbs however are of the standard finish. Well defined comb marks in the moulded light ochre hair are brought from a central crown at the back with a side parting in front and brush strokes at the temples. Eyebrows are dark ochre as are the eyelines. The lid lines, eye dots, nose dots and lips are light vermillion. The eyes are pale blue with the iris set high against the eyeline. The bisque lower arms are exceptionally long, requiring only small cloth upper sections. Although the fingers of the hands are well defined they are without thumbs and would make equally suitable right or left arms. The legs wear glossy grey/black ankle boots with light brown soles. The quality and decoration of the limbs bear no comparison with the excellence of the head.

The doll is dressed in black and white wool dog-tooth-check trousers and a black serge jacket that can best be described as a cross between a Norfolk shirt and a tunic. It has three box pleats in front and three behind and is belted at the waist with a black ribbon and a buckle improvised by two vertical rows of four black beads. The jacket is trimmed at the neck, hem and cuffs with black silk ribbon edging and a collar is just visible above the jackets neckline. A violet bow (a garish colour so dear to the hearts of Victorians in the 80's) is the sole touch of colour on this typically proprietous masculine outfit. Happily his checkered trousers serve to draw a veil over the unlikely feature of painted pink garter bows at the top of his white bisque legs!

During the 1880's the vogue for beards gradually declined and towards the close of the decade were confined to professional men and the elders. Sir Horace married late in life and at the time that this doll was dressed in representation of him in informal morning attire, he was 67 years of age. He was Architect and Surveyor to the City of London, so he had a two-fold reason for wearing this somewhat outmoded style of facial hair. He designed many buildings of importance and together with Sir John Wolfe-Barry designed London's Tower Bridge — a project he did not live to see completed in 1895.

Fig 24. 8½in (22cm). Man doll labelled 'My Dada at breakfast'. (Courtesy Elsie Potter)

1880-1890   Tamzine Billing

Fig 25. 6¾in (17cm). This doll is labelled 'Auntie Godmother bringing my dollies'. (Courtesy Elsie Potter)

Fig 25. 6¾in (17cm) high, this doll is labelled "Auntie Godmother bringing my Dollies" and represents Tamzine Billing herself. It is perplexing that she should have selected a doll cast in the image of a child for this self portrayal at the age of sixty-sive! Was a little escapist nostalgia indulged in, or was the selection left to her niece whose favourite aunt may well have been viewed through a truth-blotting rosy glow? One may perhaps hazard a guess that Aunt Tammy's choice was governed by the dolls available for dressing and this theory is substantiated by the forcible expression given to the doll in likeness of Sir Horace, her brother, which she dressed with such an eye to detail. This same concern with accuracy has certainly been employed in the execution of her own dress and accessories.

The mode of hairstyle displayed on this lightly tinted bisque shoulder head is now popularly known as the Alice-in-Wonderland hairdo. John Tenniels' illustrations for Lewis Carroll's book first published in 1865 caught the imagination of Victorian parents, and the Alice hairstyle became universally adopted for little girls, and continues in popularity now lending its name to any brand that holds the hair back from the face. The doll's moulded coiffeur is pale ochre with brushmarks all round the face where the hair is drawn back and held by a painted black ribbon terminating behind exposed ears. The back hair falls in wide vertical comb marks. The dark ochre eyebrows are uncommonly thick. The eyes of cobalt blue are painted high against black lid lines. The lips and nose dots are vermillion and the cheeks rosy. The modelling of the features is of a high standard with well defined ears, upper and lower eyelids, and a rounded plump chin.

The doll's lower limbs are her most remarkable feature. The arms terminate in beautifully sculptured child-like hands shaped with a regard for reality which is extremely rare in dolls of this tiny size. The plump legs are attractively decorated with a band of painted red ribbon loops adorning white glazed mid-calf socks and the doll wears heeled grape lustre ankle boots with soles of gold lustre. Her clothes consist of a black brocade dolman jacket beautifully worked and trimmed with black lace, fringing and beads. It is a perfect scale model of this delightful outergarment. No dart or seam is missing that would be present in its life sized counterpart! Beneath the jacket the doll wears a violet-blue dress which is no less complicated in its construction. The straight long sleeves and high neck are lace trimmed and the skirt has a front panel horizontally tucked from hem to waist, with a deep flounce at the back which is bustled. Beneath the dress there is a cotton petticoat, and matching knee length drawers, and between these a second petticoat of red barege. Over her right arm hangs a covered basket slung from a violet ribbon and a home-made umbrella made from a tapered stick wound round with brown ribbon.

Miss Sale

1880~1890

Fig 26 is 6¾in high (17cm) with a hat moulded in one with the shoulder head. The doll is labelled "Godmama" and is known to represent a Miss Sale but as no photographs of this lady have been found it is not possible to judge how much attention has been given to represent her personal characteristics. The doll is extremely fine in every detail. The bisque and decoration is of a high standard. The painter followed with accuracy the cleanly chiselled features with no trace of the all too common overlap and the equally annoying practice of decorators leaving untinted areas of moulded hair which results in an apparently thicker neck and shorter coiffeur.

The cheeks are lightly flushed on a white ground. Blue eyes are cast slightly upwards under black eyelines, and eye dots and nose dots are of light carmine. The mount is painted the same shade with a good deal of expression which together with the upward glancing eyes give the head a charmingly thoughtful appearance. Her face is slender and mature with a straight Grecian-type nose. The hair is waved all over, covering the ears and suggesting the whole is encased in a fine net. This day-wear style was prevalent in France during the early 1860's when the practice of having cauls made up from ones own hair was popular. The moulded coiffeur is a rich deep brown colour of high gloss, eyebrows being a lighter sepia tone. The doll's yellow hat is low crowned with a circular narrow brim turned slightly downwards, with a painted black ribbon and in the front two moulded feathers and a rose, encircled by five leaves. The larger of the two feathers is gold and grape lustre, the smaller one and the rose being in two tones of pink. The doll's lower limbs are of white bisque, the arms with very small well modelled hands and the legs wearing grey-black flat ankle boots with light brown soles.

She wears a sleeveless three quarter length black satin mantle trimmed with black lace at the hem and armholes. Smocked from the neckline to the shoulders, the mantle is tight fitting to the waist and fastened down the front with three magenta ribbon bows which are repeated at the inner armhole edges and in the small of the back, where the mantle puffs out to accommodate a bustle. The dress in fact has no bustle and is conceived with elegant simplicity. The material is pale grey silk taffeta with a blue stripe cut horizontally across the skirt and sleeves. A deep flounce at the hem has been worked diagonally making a most effective contrast. The doll's right arm is tucked into a small muff of black panne velvet. Her undergarments consist of knee length drawers, a red barege petticoat and one of white cotton. A delightful finishing touch is the stitching together of her legs in a walking position with the right foot well in front of the left — an apt detail for a doll dressed in outdoor garments!

Fig 26. 6¾in (17cm). This doll, with a hat moulded in one with the shoulder head, is labelled 'Godmama'. (Courtesy Elsie Potter)

1880-1890   Lady Jones

Fig 27. 6¾in (17cm). Doll labelled 'My Mama at breakfast'. (Courtesy Elsie Potter)

Fig 27. 6¾in (17cm) with a shoulder head of pink tinted glazed porcelain the doll is labelled "My Mama at Breakfast" and represents Lady Jones. She is simply dressed in a two-piece dress of corded dark blue silk with a raised leaf pattern of ultramarine and black trimmed with lace at the v-shaped neck, cuffs and hem. The jacket bodice with basques cut in one, short in front, longer and square shaped at the back — is "fastened" with seven small gold beads and the basques are trimmed with black fringing. A single violet bow decorates the front of the dress at the neck. The sleeves have been made in the vogue of the mid-80's — set-in, lightly padded, not quite reaching the wrists and finished with a frill. Undergarments consist of a full tucked cotton petticoat trimmed with pillow lace, a second petticoat of red barege and tucked cotton knee length drawers.

The quality of the doll is poor — definition of modelling is vague and the decoration slipshod. Black painted hair is centre parted with waved side puffs covering the ears. There are two rows of curls forming a ledge from ear to ear in the back. The brows and eyelines are black with eyes of such a light blue as to be barely visible. The cheeks are rouged and the mouth and nose dots painted with a lamentable lack of symmetry. The body is beige cloth and the lower limbs white bisque. The doll has two right arms (a common fault) and the lower legs have painted black ankle boots with slightly raised heels.

Although this specimen's poor quality is sharply spotlighted in the presence of her companion dolls, photographs of Lady Jones suggest the choice was not made without consideration! Others found in Horatia's dolls' house representing "Mama" in different outfits are all of glazed porcelain and this distinction applies to dolls representing this lady alone — all other members of the family and household being represented in bisque!

Ann Elizabeth Jones appears in photographic portraits with a praiseworthy, well scrubbed face, and in 1886 her figure had attained to a full development which showed small sacrifice in the interest of fashion. Photographs from her girlhood show the same severe hairstyle still worn by her some twenty years later. Her distinctive sideways smile, evident in most of her pictures is uncannily reflected in this doll's hastily executed mouth, and the faded blue eyes — while undoubtedly being a fault in the enamel, are a truthful testimony of the pale eyes that gaze from the sepia prints. There can be little doubt that a good deal of observation tempered with a touch of humour went into the selection of this doll for the representation of this lady.

Horatia Jones

1880-1890

Fig 28 is a dainty 3½in (10cm) white bisque doll labelled "Horatia in a Day Cosy Tippett". She wears a knee length blue dress of the same material as that worn by her mother with straight long sleeves, tied at the waist with a violet sash arranged in a large bow at the back. Her shoulder cape and toque are of black plush and a small violet ribbon adorns the toque with another at the neck of the tippet. Long drawers edged with a border of tatting are visible below the dress and the doll also wears a white cotton petticoat and an under-petticoat of red barege.

What is visible of her moulded hair beneath the glued on toque suggests the shoulder head may have been marketed equally in the likeness of a boy or girl. The style is short, wavey and leaves the ears exposed. The colour is high gloss dark brown. The decoration of the face is very delicate and competently painted. The blue eyes have black eyelines and dark brown eyebrows. The mouth and nose dots are precisely painted and there are subtle blush marks on the cheeks. The lower limbs are long and well shaped. Both hands and feet are finely modelled with pointed grey boots with flat heels and light tan soles.

While the doll bears no resemblance to her human counterpart at the age of ten, nor apparently has any attempt been made to select a doll with a coiffeur in likeness of Horatia's long light brown hair, the general impression nevertheless reflects some characteristics of the young Miss Jones. It is known from the outfit she wore to court in 1886 when her father received his knighthood from Queen Victoria, that she was tall for her age, extremely thin and with remarkably small hands and feet. The doll then is constant to her silhouette and the timerous little bisque face conveys a certain reality when matched against the self conscious expression in all Horatia's early photographs.

Fig 28. 3½in (10cm). White bisque doll labelled 'Horatia in a day cosy tippet'. (Courtesy Elsie Potter)

1880-1890

Peg-wooden baby and Gentleman

Fig 29 is a ¾in (2cm) peg-wooden dressed in baby robes of white muslin measuring 5¼in in length and elaborately trimmed with blue silk ribbon and very fine rose red feather stitching. The robe is tightly gathered at the waist and neckline and has ribbon rosettes on each shoulder and another with streamers at the back. The doll was commercially dressed in the 1880's when extremely long infant clothes were general and often very fanciful. Undergarment is a tucked red flannel petticoat embroidered at the hem with two rows of back stitch.

This tiny doll with her smooth head and hair painted in black wavey lines has simple facial features of a very light tone. Her legs are missing and it is tempting to suppose that specimens either made without legs or damaged in transit were priced as "seconds" thus leaving room for additional expenditure in the form of lavish dressmaking. This would have served at once to conceal the missing limbs and justify the cost of a basically incomplete article.

Fig 29. ¾in (2cm). A peg-wooden doll dressed in baby robes of white muslin (Courtesy Dorothy Coleman)

Fig 30. 5½in (14cm). A young Victorian gentleman, of high grade bisque. The hat is moulded in one with the head. (Author's Collection)

Fig 30. This 5½in (14cm) doll depicts a young Victorian gentleman. The shoulder head of high grade bisque is tinted a naturalistic flesh colour with slightly flushed cheeks and crisply delineated features. The top hat is moulded in one with the head and is painted black with a raised ribbon band and a brim dipping in front and in the back. The painted brown eyebrows are thick and the finely modelled walrus moustache is a dark glossy brown with comb marks. Beneath this is a barely visible red lower lip. Blue eyes have black eyelines and the doll has no side whiskers. The lower arms, also of flesh tinted bisque, have small cupped hands with fingers and thumbs represented. The white bisque legs are decorated with moulded ribbed hose and he wears black Hessian boots with yellow soles. The body and upper limbs are of pink cloth. The high necked white linen shirt is fastened down the back with hooks and eyes and the doll wears a blue cravat and matching blue trousers. His coat is of the short Chesterfield type — double breasted and made of black felt with collar, lapels and cuffs of velvet. It is trimmed with fine thread to simulate the braid edging associated with this mode of outergarment.

Little girl and Man doll

1880-1890

Fig 31. 3½in (9cm). Doll with tinted bisque shoulder-head and white bisque lower limbs. (Private Collection)

Fig 31 is 3½in high (9cm) with a lightly tinted bisque shoulder head with white bisque lower limbs and a white cloth body. The modelling, decoration and clothing are of an almost mediocre simplicity but, as so surprisingly often happens, the combination results in an irrefutable charm. The naivety of the product in its home-sewn outfit endows it with a special appeal.

The head is that of a little girl though the model in fact differs little from the doll in Fig 25. The café-au-lait moulded hair is totally amorphous without brush strokes or comb marks but the paint has been carried down low in front suggesting a beguiling "pudding-basin" cut with a black Alice band. The smiling mouth is light red and there are nose dots of the same tone. The eyes are large and bright blue with completely horiztonal black eyelines and brows to match the hair colour. Lower arms and hands are disproportionately large while the lower legs are short and the feet tiny! The doll wears flat heeled moulded black ankle boots with light tan soles. Her Kate Greeneway-type white muslin dress is a simple shift drawn in at the neck and under the arms without sleeves and with a blue silk ribbon sash which exactly matches the doll's eyes.

Fig 32 is a 6in (15cm) doll with a white cloth body, untinted lower limbs and shoulder head of bisque, the latter with a fine naturalistic complexion coating. The head alone is illustrated for its singularity and luxuriant beard. His black painted hair is waved in layers with comb marks radiating from the crown with no parting. The beard has brush strokes along the line of the cheeks and at the barely defined ears. The doll's sideburns descend across the cheeks, merge with the moustache and join the beard, giving him a thoroughly bewhiskered appearance! The black paint is high gloss and is repeated on the eye lines, pupils and eyebrows. Eyes are painted brown and a dark red lower lip shows beneath the moustache.

Clairty of modelling is not of the standard one would expect of such good quality bisque and suggests that the mould have become worn by the time this specimen was cast from it. In favour of this theory is the fact that beards were no longer commonplace for young men in the 1880's whereas resplendant growths of facial hair were in full swing throughout the 70's, when side whiskers, beards and moustaches were worn in great variety and any combination. Some arguments against this assumption however must be that for a mould to deteriorate considerably before being finally discarded the product must have been a popular seller, and the rarity of this doll disputes this factor. Also the statement that beards became demodé at a given time is only true in so far as their general popularity is concerned and an isolated example can be cited for almost any fashion throughout every age. The tantalising unconcern on the part of doll manufacturers for recorded data about their products makes all speculation ever open to divergent opinions. One is fortunate to know in this instance the date of purchase (1885) and to have been given the opportunity for including such a highly individual doll in this book.

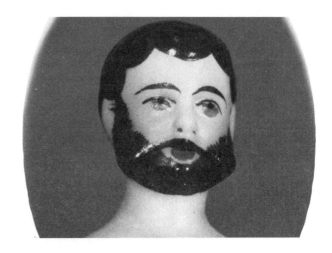

Fig 32. 6in (15cm). Man doll. The head alone is illustrated for its singularity and luxuriant beard. (Courtesy Moira Garland)

1880-1890 'Prince Charming'

Fig 33. A good quality man doll dressed to represent Prince Charming. His somewhat encumbent outfit is of pink and green sateen comprising breeches, waistcoat, a jacket and cloak, the latter two decorated with green feather stitching. There is lace trim at the wrists and knees and glass beads adorn all his garment. The doll was dressed by Anna Tribe for her stepdaughter Nell between 1885 and 1890 and is now in the collection of Nell Tribe's niece.

One can guess the doll's height to have been 5½in (14cm); his lower limbs are alas all missing. The stuffed body is of white cloth and the beautifully detailed pink tinted shoulder head has distinctive paintwork. The café-au-lait moulded hair is centre parted from the front to the nape of the neck and there are comb marks delineating the waved style. Although the hair, moustache and eyebrows are all the same colour, only the moustache has a glossy finish and this too has comb marks. Its unswept ends have embued the doll with an amused air and this is further enhanced by bright blue eyes literally sparkling with gloss and painted glancing to the right. There are black eyelines, red nose dots and a lower lip visible. The modelling of the whole head and detail of features is well defined. Furthermore the head is interesting in that it reflects the transitional stage from the uncompromising Victorian male image to the more benevolent father figure developing towards the approaching 90's.

Fig 33. A good quality man doll dressed to represent Prince Charming, he was dressed between 1885 and 1890. Lower limbs missing. Stuffed body of white cloth. Pink tinted shoulder head. (Courtesy Stella Burrell)

1890~1900

1890-1900 — Grandfather doll

Fig 34. 5¼in (13cm). 'Grandfather' is modelled in representation of an elderly man. Pink tinted bisque shoulder head. White lower limbs. Feet wearing black painted ankle boots with small heels and tan soles. (Author's Collection)

Fig 34. At the turn of the century a new group of dolls' house dolls were produced in Germany which scored an immediate success and marked a whole new range conceived in objective terms. Balding and wrinkled old men, greyhaired ladies, cosily attractive mothers and fathers, and children at last displaying a harmony of scale beside the adult dolls. Nannies, cooks, footmen, housemaids, butlers and coachmen were all mass-produced and impeccably up to date. A further innovation in the design of these dolls was the inclusion of wire inside the cloth upper arm sections enabling them to be bent into varying positions. The popularity of these dolls' house dolls ensured their continued production well into the twentieth century.

"Grandfather" is 5¼in (13cm) high and is modelled in representation of an elderly man. This mould when found commercially dressed is often in the role of a butler or gardener, but the specimen shown here has been raised to the position of Grandpapa. Dressed in a loose black silk robe-de-chambre edged with violet braid, it is caught in front with a silver buckle hinting of the one time presence of a belt. He wears trousers of dark brown linen and at his neck is a black bow tie stitched to a shirt that is his only commercially made garment.

The bisque shoulder head is pink tinted, and the lower limbs are white with feet wearing black painted ankle boots with small heels and tan soles. The face has painted blue eyes with black eyelines, gray brows and a smiling mouth and nose dots of light orange. Wrinkle lines are painted in grey strokes from the corners of the mouth, nose and eyes, with three horizontal lines across the forehead. The top of the head is bald with grey moulded hair commencing low at the back, appearing in the front just above the ears and continuing down to moulded, painted side whiskers. By the 90's side whiskers worn without other facial hair had become the distinguishing marks of menials, but the casual grandeur of this fine old gentleman's informal attire, steers him safely round the awkward corner of the social mix-up!

Grandmother doll

1890-1900

Fig 35. 4¾in (12cm). 'Grandmama' is dressed in black trimmed with lace. Pink tinted shoulder head with moulded grey hair and matching eyebrows. (Author's Collection)

Fig 35, 4¾in (12cm), is dressed as a dolls' house Grandmama but is found equally often in the guise of a cook. This appealing elderly lady doll has a pink tinted bisque shoulder head with moulded painted grey hair and matching eyebrows. Wrinkle lines are painted on the forehead, at the corners of the eyes and at the nose and mouth. Her blue eyes have black eyelines and the lips and nose dots are light orange. Hair is centre parted with side puffs covering the ears and with a chignon at the back and a black painted and moulded comb visible above.

The black dress is lace trimmed at the neck and sleeves and is an extremely well made piece of home dressmaking. The front panel of the skirt is gathered with a flounced hemline. The back has the upward jutting bustle of the 80's which contrasted considerably with the softer lines of the bustle from the previous decade. Beneath this the back of the skirt is box pleated and elongated to form a short train. The dress is belted at the waist and has a beautifully made buckle of silver beads. The sleeves are the "Leg o' Mutton" type. It is probable that this mid-80's vogue of dress is a decade or so earlier than the doll but, as befits a grandmother, will have been suitably demodé at the time she was dressed. The doll's pink cloth body has wired upper arms and white bisque lower limbs. She wears black painted ankle boots with heels and tan-coloured soles.

1890-1900   # Dolls' House Papa

Fig 36. 5¼in (13cm). Man doll, here representing a dolls' house Papa. Pink tinted bisque shoulder head with good facial modelling. (Author's Collection)

Fig 36 is a brown-eyed man doll here representing a dolls' house papa but found in innumerable varieties of dress. The specimen has been found in all kinds of domestic livery and also military uniforms. Judging by the large numbers remaining, this versatile doll seems to have enjoyed a long production run. His features reflect the changes that had formed in the late nineteenth century in terms of human relations and specifically the old concept of parents as remote beings. Gone is the cold reserve and here rendered in miniature is a member of the new less conventional generation.

The doll stands 5¼in (13cm) high with a pink tinted bisque shoulder head and good facial modelling. His glossy black painted hair is centre parted from the forehead to the nape of the neck with strong comb marks and brush strokes at the temples. The moulded moustache is black but without comb marks. Eyes are large and light brown with black eyelines and eyebrows. Nose dots and lower lip are brick red. The ears have good detail and stand well away from the head. He wears a black Norfolk type belted jacket over brown and white check trousers. White collar and cuffs show at the neck and wrists and a jaunty red bow tie is stitched to the collar. A large marcasite buckle is sewn to the belt and a watch chain of silver beads is stitched to the right front of the jacket. The body is pink cloth with wired upper arms and white bisque lower limbs. Hands are fairly shapeless but with fingers defined. Lower legs wear mid-calf heeled boots painted black with yellow soles.

Dolls' House Mama

1890-1900

Fig 37a,b is 5½in (14cm) high and dressed as a dolls' house mama in green embroidered silk. The material is considerably earlier than the doll as is very often the case with dolls dressed in the home from rag bags containing scraps from earlier generations. Everything else about her points to the closing years of the nineteenth century.

The fashion features of this decade were rather more precise than the collective styles of the 70's and 80's. Hair was worn long and tied in a knot with a frizzy fringe. The bustle had gone for good but there was still the tendency for interest to be focused on the back of the skirt which was sometimes trained. Dresses were tight fitting and flaired at the hem. Necklines were high with much interest centred on the yoke, the sleeves were tight with fullness at the shoulders. The doll can be seen to faithfully reflect the female silhouette of 1895.

Her pink tinted bisque shoulder head has a café-au-lait moulded coiffeur with the short front hair arranged in curls

Fig 37a. 5½in (14cm). Doll dressed as a dolls' house Mama in green embroidered silk. Pink tinted shoulder head with café-au-lait moulded coiffeur. (Private Collection)

Fig 37b

on the forehead and the main weight of long hair being waved, puffed and drawn up into a coiled knot. The ears are exposed as was the vogue in this period. Her painted blue eyes are large, covering the whole area within the socket with black eyelines and eyebrows matching the hair colour. Lips and nose dots are light orange and lower limbs are white bisque. Feet are very small and wear black painted ankle boots with heels. The dolls body is of pink cloth and the upper arms are wired. The doll has been dressed with the slick assurance of a good dressmaker. The yoke is constructed from braiding of needle made lace with picot edging. The sash is of red and silver tinsel ribbon tied in the back with streamers hanging to the hemline. The hem is decorated with medallions of Irish crochet lace and a flounce of green linen. A particularly delightful feature is the chatelaine at the doll's waist. It is of gilded metal and comprises scissors, key, button hook and pen-knife.

1890-1900 Boy doll

Fig 38. 3½in (9cm). Endearing boy doll with a shoulder head of pink tinted bisque and lower limbs of white bisque. (Author's Collection)

Fig 38. This endearing boy doll measures 3½in (9cm) with a shoulder head of pink tinted bisque and lower limbs of white bisque. On the legs the white has been painted out with ink to simulate black hose and the added colour has been continued on the cloth upper legs. The blue and black side-button boots are also home additions in oil colour causing one to guess that the doll portrayed an actual child dressed for some special occasion.

The doll's cloth body is pink with wired upper arms. The moulded café-au-lait hair is curled all over and large blue eyes have black eyelines and eyebrows to match the hair. Lips and nose dots are deep orange. The success of the decoration is a happy accident rather than the result of skill. The features have been painted not without competence but with signs of haste. The head is turned slightly to the left with side glancing eyes. The incidence of the doll's left leg being shorter than the right results in a stance that heightens the disarming quality of his expression. Here is an instance of indifferent brushwork and carelessness along the assembly line resulting in a unique and charming product.

The doll is dressed in a black velvet Lord Fauntleroy suit with lace collar and cuffs tied at the waist with a silk ribbon sash. This boy's party outfit had been in use for some years before Mrs. Hodgson-Burnetts book "Little Lord Fauntleroy" published in 1886 put it firmly on the fashion map — where it has enjoyed varying degrees of popularity ever since.

Girl doll

1890-1900

Fig 39. 3½in (9cm). A girl doll dressed ready for a party, her hairstyle is typical of the 1890's. Pink bisque shoulder head. The body is pink cloth with wired upper arms and white bisque lower arms. (Author's Collection)

Fig 39 is a girl doll with a hairstyle typical of the 1890's. During this decade the vogue for knots, braided, coiled or waved worn on the top of the head was "all the rage" for women and girls alike. Some versions were quite elaborate — particularly those designed for evening wear, but this dolls style is in a fittingly simplified juvenile form. Her silk dress of gathered tucks is not distinctive of any given period of the nineteenth century. The mode would not have been out of place at a children's party of the 1850's nor noticably conspicuous at such a function even today. The doll's height is 3½in (9cm) and she has moulded café-au-lait hair and a black painted band round her topknot. The exposed ears have little modelling but all other features of the pink bisque shoulder head are defined and well decorated. The blue eyes have black horizontal eyelines and eyebrows match the hair colour. Lips and nose dots are pale red. The body is pink cloth with wired upper arms and white bisque lower limbs. Feet have small black ankle boots with flat heels and white soles.

Her dress is of ivory silk and the top half of the skirt is covered by a blue ribbon trimmed at its base with lace thus effectively suggesting a dress comprised of a frilled bodice, blue skirt and deep frilled him. Underwear consists of a white cotton petticoat and knee length drawers edged with lace. This little doll has some very charming qualities not least her pensive expression and pidgeon-toed stance — once again carelessness along the assembly line.

1890-1900   # Footman

Fig 40. 5½in (14cm). Footman with well decorated features, on a fine quality bisque flesh tinted shoulder head. (Author's Collection)

Fig 40 is a 5½in (14cm) footman with well decorated features on a fine quality bisque shoulder head. He wears the centrally parted hair which was perhaps the most conspicuous Victorian vagary of masculine fashion, first appearing in the mid-nineteenth century and containing in vogue for some fifty years. The doll's side whiskers without other facial hair indicate the menial position for which he was intended to be dressed. His outfit is hand made but differs little in style, colour and trim from its commercially made equivalent; the noticable difference being the use of velvet and brocade whereas felt was general for factory made versions.

The modelling of the doll's flesh tinted head is very crisp and his rather large ears have good definition. The ochre coloured hair has comb marks both on the head and side whiskers and all the decoration including the complexion coat is assured and subtle. Eyes are blue with black eyelines, dark ochre eyebrows and light red lips and nose dots. Lower limbs are white bisque, the legs with black mid-calf boots with heels and yellow soles. These are incorrectly set into their cloth upper sections resulting in another pidgeon-toed specimen! The upper arms are wired and the body is pink cloth.

His dark red velvet jacket is fastened at the waist with a single brass button and is trimmed with gold braid. A cravat of white chiffon fills the exposed area of the open cut jacket. Breeches are of velvet and brocade with a red silk cummerbund.

Coachman

1890-1900

Fig 41a,b. A charming example of a once familiar figure — the coachman. These members of the outdoor staff were clad with much consideration to matching their liveries to the colour schemes of the carriages, and their gold or silver buttons often bore the family coat of arms. This late nineteenth century dolls' house example reflects the development of the winter livery to the later chauffeur's uniform.

The doll is 4¾in (12cm) high with a pink tinted bisque shoulder head, moulded black painted hair and moustaches with light orange lips and painted brown eyes with black eyelines. The lower limbs are of white bisque with good modelling of the hands, and legs wearing black painted boots with heels. Varnished strips of tan coloured paper have been glued to the tops to resemble the Jockey Boot.

Fig 41b

Fig 41a. 4¾in (12cm). Coachman. The doll has a pink tinted bisque shoulder head, moulded black painted hair and moustache. White bisque lower limbs with good modelling of hands. (Courtesy Kay Desmonde)

The brim of his cardboard top hat has been lost and only glue marks testify to its one time existence. The hat band is a gold paper strip as is the braid edging on his collar, cuffs and pockets of the double breasted caped Ulster with the typical half-belt back. Buttons are also gold paper. Beneath the felt maroon coloured coat the doll wears black velvet breeches. His pink cloth body has wired upper arms. He is of the same mould as the Papa Doll in Fig 36 and the role of a coachman for which he has been commercially dressed, makes a paradoxical contrast with the absence of any side whiskers and the presence of a fine moustache. However, his apparent social de-escalation merely adds humour and interest to a very pleasing specimen.

1890-1900

Children's Nurse and Coachman

Fig 42 is 5½in (14cm) high and the mould from which the head was cast is the same as was used for the mama doll in Fig.37. This specimen is commercially dressed as a children's nurse in machined linen. The dress is light blue with white cuffs, collar, apron and cap. Beneath this the doll wears cotton drawers and a petticoat. Her pink tinted bisque shoulder head has moulded café-au-lait coloured hair. The eyes are pale blue with black eyelines, dark ochre eyebrows and brick red lips and nose dots. The body is pink cloth with wired upper arms. The lower limbs are of untinted greasey bisque. Feet wear brisk red moulded shoes with heels and light yellow soles.

The doll's clothing is a good example of the differences between home-sewn and factory made clothing. The latter wrested a polished style from a minimal amount and usually lacked the richness and subtlety of the individual outfit. A point of interest about the factory dressed dolls of the late nineteenth century is the noticable tendency to ignore the social implications of hair modes. As the 90's draw to a close one sees discrepancies of hair and dress styles significantly escalating, doubtelss reflecting a relaxation in social stratification — if only at nursery level.

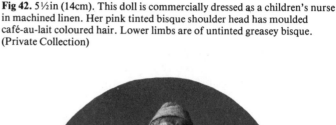

Fig 42. 5½in (14cm). This doll is commercially dressed as a children's nurse in machined linen. Her pink tinted bisque shoulder head has moulded café-au-lait coloured hair. Lower limbs are of untinted greasey bisque. (Private Collection)

Fig 43. 6in (15cm). Coachman with moulded hat. His face is a replica of that of the footman in Fig 40. (Private Collection)

Fig 43 is 6in (15cm) high from his flat ankle boots to the top of his coachman's hat. Apart from this additional moulded feature his face is a replica of the footman in Fig 40. What is visible of the doll's blond hair shows that he wears a centrally parted style with side whiskers and comb marks. The modelling of his ears, nose, mouth and eyelids is exceptionally good and detailed. Eyes are light blue with black eyelines and eyebrows are dark ochre. Lips and nostril dots are a bright reddish-brown. The hat is painted black with a raised ribbon band with the brim dipping in the front and back. His lower limbs are of untinted bisque with good modelling of the hands. The body is pink cloth with wired upper arms.

His commercially made felt outfit has black trousers and a beige double-breasted jacket embellished with gold braid and buttons.

Nanny with baby

1890-1900

Fig 44. As the nineteenth century progressed towards its closing years the size of the female head tended to increase with hair being piled over higher and brushed over pads at the sides. This 5in (13cm) doll displays an evening coiffeur which is conspicuously at variance with her nannie's uniform! The moulded style is painted dark blond with a black painted ribbon bowknot on top and two roll curls on the forehead. The sides are puffed outwards and up, and at the back there is a vertical braid descending from the bow and terminating in a small low chignon. In life the braid and chignon would be false pieces attached to the bow; roll curls and side hair of such volume using up all the wearers natural hair.

The doll's pink tinted bisque shoulder head has well modelled exposed ears and good decoration. Large blue eyes have black eyelines, dark ochre eyebrows and light orange lips and nose dots. Her lower limbs are of untinted bisque. The hands are well defined on both outer and inner sides and the legs wear painted black ankle boots with small heels and tan soles. The pink cloth body has wired upper arms. The doll's home made outfit is of black and white striped cotton with white linen collar, cuffs and belt, and a white muslin embroidered apron. Three beads are sewn to the collar in representation of buttons.

Her "charge" is of an earlier date and is a very small doll (2in high) with a hairstyle of tightly packed rows of sausage curls with a central curl on the forehead. Her long robe of muslin and lace conceals moulded ankle boots. She wears a cream satin cape with matching ribbon ties decorated with a single chiffon rosette. This is an all-bisque doll without complexion tinting. The hair is light ochre with matching eyebrows. Eyes are blue with dark ochre eyelines and a dark red smiling mouth.

Fig 44. 5in (13cm). This doll displays an evening coiffeur which is conspicuously at variance with her nannie's uniform! Her 'charge' is a very small all-bisque doll. (Author's Collection)

1890-1900　　　　　　　　　　　Twins

Fig 45. 7in (18cm) bisque shoulder head twins with bisque lower limbs shown with a layette that was hand sewn in a Belgian convent. One sees in these dolls the naturalism that was gaining a foothold in the doll manufacturing business with faces more related to legitimate human characteristics. An unsophisticated quality pervades this pair with their widely spaced eyes, uncomplicated hairstyles and innocent expressions. They gaze out through the frills and furbelows of their fine muslin gowns (over pink under-robes) with the solemn aspects of real children.

Although one might question their comparatively large scale for inclusion in a book about dolls' house dolls, it should not be forgotten that playhouses were manufactured six feet or more in height and contained furniture of a scale which sometimes tempts collectors to categorize them as apprentice pieces. These large houses were commercially made and equipped with trappings to scale and the dolls shown here were indeed found inside such a house.

Their moulded light blonde hair has distinct comb marks and the bobbed style covers the ears. Eyelids are clearly modelled and the high grade bisque has a natural complexion coat. Single stroke dark ochre eyebrows are set at a wistful angle and large cobalt blue eyes have black eyelines. Lips and nostril dots are light rose. The arms share the excellent quality and tint of the heads and the fingers and thumbs of the cupped hands are well defined. The long gowns conceal neatly shod moulded footwear. Knee length ribbed white socks and black two strap shoes with heels and yellow soles. The dolls' have pink cloth bodies of the conventional type — wasp-waisted, wide hipped and sawdust filled. An incised letter B appears low on the right back shoulder of both dolls.

Fig 45. 7in (18cm). Twins with bisque shoulder heads shown with a layette that was hand sewn in a Belgium convent. (Author's Collection)

Actress

1880-1890

Figs 46, 47 and 48 are late nineteenth century dolls, fancy-dressed to represent theatrical characters. Fig 46 is a 5in (13cm) lady doll whose moulded hair is concealed by a wig of auburn silk thread. Her painted features have additional touches of water colour as if to underline her dramatic status. These touches are centred on the eye area where lashes have been added, eyebrows thickened and the eyes enlarged. Long braids descend on either side of the wig which is otherwise styled in the fashion of the late 1890's, puffed and waved with a heavy coiled chignon and without a fringe. In life this style was built over wired pads and frames and even this detail was not overlooked by the masterly dresser of these dolls. Brown binding tape covers the moulded coiffeur, at once serving to conceal it and adding the desired volume to the wig. The doll's dress is a fanciful melée of styles but is nevertheless dominated by twelfth century fashion. The bodice tight fitting to the hips, the full skirt and long decorative girdle worn loose on the hips and hanging low in front, are all features of the last quarter of the twelfth century, as are the lengthy braids and fold band encircling the head which once secured a veil. Only wisps of this remain. All this suggests that the doll represents an actress — probably from an Arthurian legendery role. She is however a late nineteenth century doll and only the hair fashions of the day deflected the creator of this mini-Guinevere to be influenced by her contemporary ideals. The doll's green silk dress is decorated with braided gold thread. Under-garments are commercially made of starched gauze. Bisque shoulder head is incised on back: 618 12/0. Bisque lower arms have well modelled hands and legs wear black moulded boots with heels.

Fig 46. 5in (13cm). A bisque shoulder head lady doll with moulded hair which is concealed by a wig of auburn silk thread. (Courtesy Moira Garland)

1890-1900

Shakespearean Character

Fig 47 is a 6¾in (17cm) man doll of exceptional quality and colouring. His neat beard and moustaches are finely modelled and well painted in light ochre as is the hair which is parted just off centre. Probably intended to represent a Shakespearean character, the Tudor style of his costume is well observed and only the Cavalier-type hat is a later mis-match. His close fitting doublet is ivory and yellow brocade with puffed sleeves and padded breeches of peach silk. The neck ruff is of rouched chiffon ribbon and the trunk hose is ivory silk. Buckled belt and gauntlet gloves are white kid leather and a silver-paper dagger is slotted behind the belt. Shoes are embroidered-on gold thread with gold paper soles and are decorated with ribbon rosettes. The short flared cape is of grey-blue velvet with gold thread embroidery. Wide brimmed hat matches the cape and is trimmed with a single feather and ribbon rosette. With the exception of this plumed hat which is a seventeenth century feature the doll cuts a dashing figure from the last quarter of the sixteenth century.

Fig 47. 6¾in (17cm). A man doll of exceptional quality and colouring, dressed to represent a Shakespeare character. (Courtesy Moira Garland)

Tudor Gentleman

1890-1900

Fig 48 represents another Tudor gentleman but the doll used in this presentation is that most commonly found Dolls' House Papa with black painted hair, moustaches and brown eyes. Standing 6¼in (16cm) his costume is an almost exact replica of the previous doll's. Brocade doublet and silk trunk hose are identical, but breeches and sleeves are cream silk, the latter with pink ribbon bowknot decoration. A charming feature is the doll's pink girdle studded with cut glass beads which dips so low in front that it gives the perfect illusion of the Peascod-belly style. Suspended from the girdle on a narrow pink ribbon is a sheathed sword commercially made of lead. This doll's ruff has perished but traces at the back show it was also rouched chiffon. The short cape is brocade lined with pink grosgrain. Hat is brocade faced with silk and lavishly trimmed with ribbon, swansdown and feathers. Shoes are grosgrain with ribbon trim and rosettes.

These three and the following two dolls all from the same source are immaculately preserved behind, but frayed and faded in front. From this one concludes they were displayed under glass but exposed to prolonged sunlight. This is particularly marked in the bride doll (Fig 49) whose gown is completely perished on one side where continuous angled sunshine eventually broke down the silk fibres. Whoever dressed these dolls for whatever purpose quite rightly deemed them worthy of exhibition. Clearly they spent many years as charming decorative objects, but sadly near a sunny window.

Fig 48. 6¼in (16cm). A commonly found man doll dressed to represent a Tudor gentleman (Courtesy Moira Garland)

1890-1900　　　　　Bridal pair

Fig 49. 6¼in (16cm). Bridegroom doll with fine paintwork on a good quality bisque shoulder head. (Courtesy Moira Garland)

Fig 50. 6in (15cm). Bride doll with an auburn silk thread wig. Dressed in ivory silk decorated with braid and lace. (Courtesy Moira Garland)

Figs 49 and 50 are a late nineteenth century bridal pair, the bride with a wig of auburn silk thread and additional water colour eye make-up as with Fig 46. Standing 6in (15cm) the doll evinces all the fashion details of the closing years of the 1890's. The princess line trained dress with its focal point at the corsage, high neck, wasp waist and full length tight sleeves that replaced the immensely full sleeve of the early 90's. The skilfully made wig also slots fashionably into the closing years of the century with its puffed waves, heavy coiled chignon and the absence of a fringe which was demodé by 1896.

Much detailed work has been put into the presentation of this miniature bridal doll. Dressed in ivory silk decorated with braid and a full length front panel of lace. Yoke, sleeves and veil are of net. Decorative trim and bouquet are white millinery flowers and dried grass. Underwear comprises three cotton petticoats of which the uppermost is elaborately tucked, lace trimmed and threaded with blue ribbon. Cloth body with bisque lower limbs. Small well defined hands and tiny feet wearing black moulded boots.

Her bridegroom is a 6¼in (16cm) doll with centre parted moulded hair and moustaches of the handle-bar type. Fine paintwork on a good quality bisque shoulder head. His rather hefty appearance results from the bisque lower limbs terminating in large hands with free standing thumbs and exceptionally big feet in tall black painted boots. This model is often found commercially dressed in military uniform. The specimen here was dressed in the home in a black felt tailcoat suit, gauze shirt, starched linen collar and white bow tie. His single breasted waistcoat is beautifully made of silk canvas with three applied buttons. The top hat is cardboard covered with black sateen and with a silk ribbon band.

These dolls are of an earlier design than the fashions they exhibit with such exactness. Beneath the bride's silken wig is concealed the moulded frizzy-fringed coiffeur largely abandoned by the time her dress style came into vogue. The groom's hairstyle reflects a similar mis-match as side partings for men were general by the turn of the century.

All-Bisque dolls

All-Bisque

All-Bisque dolls

In the third quarter of the nineteenth century a miniature doll appeared on the toyshop scene constructed on quite different lines to the cloth bodies variety. This type now known as the All-Bisque is generally considered to have been manufactured in France and Germany concurrently, and later also in Japan. Whether they were initially intended as dolls' house inhabitants or, as has been suggested of the earlier specimens, Child Fashion Dolls, is a point of conjecture. Nevertheless large numbers have come to light inside dolls' houses and they were clearly used by children for dolls' house play and so I think appropriately fall within the scope of this book. Only a few examples are included here, however, as this field has already been extensively researched and documented by Genevieve Angoine in her book "All-Bisque and Half-Bisque Dolls."

As the word coined for this type implies all its components were made of bisque, with a lovely patina simulating juvenile complexions both in colouring and texture. The head, torso, arms and legs were made separately and strung together with elastic, tape or wire, giving articulation at the neck, shoulders and hips. A rare varient has its limbs in two sections with bisque ball joints giving additional mobility at the elbows and knees. A less sophisticated design has the head and body moulded in one; these are dubbed by collectors as Stiff-Necks. There is also the Swing-Hip — a rare type in any size and very scarce in miniature. These are stiff-neck dolls with cloth between the bisque sections at the waist and leg tops allowing for some movement. Their arms are elastic, strung through shoulder sockets in the usual manner.

Mostly all-bisques have wigs of mohair or animal skin over an open crown, ball-head of flat-topped solid crown with or without stringing holes. Glass eyes are stationary or of the counterweight sleep type. These dolls are also found with painted eyes and moulded hairstyles. Modelled shoes and ribbed hose decorated in a variety of colour combinations are a particularly charming feature. Bare footed specimens are more rare with the exception of the Frozen Charlottes where the reverse is true. These dolls usually represent a child and this is more often a girl than a boy.

All-Bisque "children" continued in production into the twentieth century but their peak of quality and sophistication was reached in the early 1880's when they were sold commercially dressed in splendid silks and satins excessively decorated with lace, shirred ribbons and nosegays of artificial flowers. Numbers are found in fancy dress and regional clothes and more rarely coloured specimens in ethnic costume. The all-bisque doll was manufactured in a wide range of sizes, some so minute as to find ready acceptance in the dolls' house nursery as the toy dolls of dolls!

'Teenage' doll

All-Bisque

For anyone believing the "teenage doll" to be a twentieth century innovation, Fig 51a and b must surely dispel this long perpetuated myth. The doll's proportions are child-like and her cascading double tied hairstyle is a juvenile fashion of the late 1870's, but her costume emulates the adult mode of this period and beneath the jacket is a moulded adolescent bosom emphasised by blush marks.

This exceptionally well preserved all-bisque stands 6in (15cm) high. The solid dome head is held in the kid lined neck socket by the original rubber stringing doubled over wooden bar inside the head, the two ends emerging through the open neck into the torso and through stringing exit holes to the legs where they are wedged with glued pegs. The arms are strung horizontally through the torso and secured in the same way. They are long and straight with quite large hands of which each finger is delineated with pink brush strokes. Her slender legs wear mid-calf white painted socks with a ribbed pattern moulded in the bisque. High heeled two strap shoes are painted powder blue with light brown soles.

The fine textured bisque is tinted with superb delicacy. The features are well proportioned and the decoration skilful. The lips and nose dots are a light rose colour and the closed mouth is painted smiling. Blush marks on the cheeks are beautifully gradated into the complexion coat. Single stroke eyebrows are dark ochre. The doll's protruding fixed glass eyes are of such a deep ultramarine that her black pupils being only a shade darker are barely discernable. The eyelashes are painted commencing with a dot and tapering to a fine point. Her long blonde hair is heavily be-ribboned with blue silk. One ribbon band encircles the head and is tied and stitched into a multi-looped bow together with a bunch of pink millinery flowers. A second ribbon is tied level with the neck and a third at the base of the hair. The wig is mounted on a gauze cap and is her only feature to have suffered the ravages of time. Small tufts at the temples remain to testify to a lost fringe which would have framed and softened the forehead and which undoubtedly fell victim to moth.

The doll's day dress in the fashion of 1876 is a truly sumptuous creation. Hand sewn of light blue silk it comprises the tie-back style trained dress with matching jacket, both edged with shirred ribbon and lace. The ribbon and flower decoration in the doll's hair is repeated on the front of the jacket and on the front panel of the skirt. There is another ribbon bowknot low at the back on the train. Undergarments are of starched buckram and consist of a trained lace edged petticoat and drawers. On her head the doll wears a linen hat trimmed and decorated with satin ribbon of the same shade of blue as her dress and shoes.

This doll is particularly notable for the high standards which pervade all her aspects — the distinctive bisque, the artistic decoration, her beautiful eyes, sweet expression and graceful stance. The protective kid liners placed at her five points of articulation, the detail in the well proportioned limbs, the striking wig and outstanding dress all sustain a degree of excellence.

Fig 51a. 6in (15cm). Exceptionally well preserved all-bisque doll with solid dome head. She wears a day dress in the fashion of 1876. (Author's Collection)

Fig 51b

All-Bisque Peg-strung doll

Fig 52a. 6in (15cm). Peg strung all-bisque with solid dome head. Her professionally made clothes are in the prevailing fashion of the early 1880's. (Author's Collection)

Fig 52b

Fig 52a and b. A 6in (15cm) All-Bisque, individual for her fine peach coloured bisque and lovely oval face. As with most early examples preserved in good condition her professionally made clothes display great skill. She is peg strung with elastic from a wooden bar inside her ball head. Her large fixed eyes are threaded blue-grey encircled with Prussian blue with black painted eyelines and upper and lower lashes. The modelling of the features is very good and the ears particularly are modelled in unusualy good detail. Her wig is light blonde mohair which was originally dressed in a single heavy braid, but its condition is now too frail for any attempt to restore the style. The wig is mounted on a linen cap of the kind more usually found on larger dolls.

The faded blue buckrum lined sateen dress is unpretentious but pays its debt to the prevailing fashion of the early 1880's. The low waist and pleated skirt, the lace trim delineating the lines of the mode, the silk bows on the shoulders — all relate to the period. The small forward tilting straw hat is decorated with a white feather and blue ribbon. Five silk bound buttons of pale grey decorate the front of the dress though the opening is at the back secured by two diminutive hooks and eyes. The short sleeves tell us that this is a party dress. Underwear consists of a pleated lace trimmed buckrum petticoat and drawers. Both have drawstrings at the waist and all the clothes are removable. The doll's long straight legs have orange mid-calf socks with clear modelling of their vertically ribbed texture. The high heeled two strap shoes are painted black with tan soles.

Small plump girl

All-Bisque

Fig 53. 6in (15cm). This all-bisque doll has counterweight sleep eyes and an open crown sealed with a plaster dome. (Author's Collection)

Fig 53 is another superlative All-Bisque of the early 80's, a period which is unequalled for the consistently high standard of this doll type. This 6in (15cm) doll has counterweight sleep eyes with waxed eyelids and the open crowd is sealed with a plaster dome. Her blonde mohair wig is mounted on a gauze cap. The face is modelled with great delicacy; the snub nose and smiling lips being conceived with a perfect appreciation of that stage between infancy and girlhood. Here we see the product of a decade which produced the most polished and sophisticated little-girl-dolls with their fashions and even their facial characteristics paying debt to the Parisian current fashions.

The doll has thin multi-stroke feathered eyebrows and upper and lower eyelashes. The glass sleep eyes are navy blue. A small aperture, barely wide enough to allow the doubled over elastic to pass through from the head is situated at the base of the neck, which fits into a kid lined socket. The peg strung arms and legs also have kid washers at their points of articulation and are beautifully fashioned with creases at the elbows and wrists, and equally the thighs, knees and calves of her legs are most realistically conceived. The torso is modelled with uninhibited naturalism and the whole gives a charming effect of a considerably overweight small girl! The palms of her hands are fleshy and every finger is individually shaped. Moulded finger nails give a final touch of quality workmanship. Fat legs appear to be almost bursting out of tall four strap boots with square heels and tan soles, and the white mid-calf socks have a circle of lilac at the top.

Her low waisted pink satin party frock has a close fitting box pleated bodice. The short double skirt is also pleated and is distended by a flounced petticoat and the whole is lined with buckrum. The dress is lace trimmed at the yoke, shoulders, bodice and skirt and is a commercially made product of considerable flair.

All-Bisque

Dome head doll and Frozen Charlotte

Fig 54. 4in (10cm). Peg strung with solid dome head with articulation at the neck, shoulder and hips. (Courtesy Marée Tarnowska)

Fig 55. 4in (10cm). All bisque 'Frozen Charlotte'. Her ball head has the remnants of a blonde mohair wig. Clearly defined face features with good decoration. (Private Collection)

Fig 54 is a 4in (10cm) doll that has not been conceived in the perfectionist spirit of the previous three. However, the defects in her bisque and lack of clarity of modelling are outweighed by the individuality of her face. Possibly of French origin, her closely set elongated eyes suggest an earlier date than her coat-dress of the 1880's. She is peg strung from a solid dome head with articulation at the neck, shoulders and hips. The bisque is pale and the small pursed lips are light orange with nose and eye dots of the same colour. Her eyelashes have been painted not in the usual single stroke way but as a continuous wavy line on both upper and lower lids. Dark ochre eyebrows almost meet at the bridge of the nose. The bulbous blue eyes are inset and have large pupils. The light blonde mohair wig is on a gauze cap. The slender straight arms have well formed hands and legs wear mid-calf white socks and blue two strap high heeled shoes.

Her princess style coat-dress may well not be her original outfit as the doll came to light in a collection of All-Bisques with an assortment of clothes, from which a dress was selected to fit her size. It is of blue silk trimmed with shirred ribbon and lace with a ribbon bowknot fastened in front.

Fig 55. Frozen Charlottes are frequently found in bisque and the quality of early specimens is superlative both in texture and decoration. The doll shown here has been re-dressed and may well not have owned an original garment, as the large numbers found without clothes coupled with their descriptive term Bathing Doll implies that they were for the main part sold undressed.

This 4in (17cm) bisque Frozen Charlotte has a pale complexion and feels dry and porous to the touch but is without any roughness. Her ball head has the remnants of a blonde mohair wig. The features of the face are clearly defined and the decoration is good. Cobalt blue painted eyes have large pupils with eyelines and eyebrows of dark ochre. The smiling mouth is pale orange. Her slim bent arms have slightly cupped down-turned hands with finely modelled fingers and thumbs on the upper side only. The slender legs have very well modelled feet and toes.

Girl doll with original clothing

All-Bisque

Fig 56 is a 6in (15cm) All-Bisque girl doll immaculately preserved in her original clothing. She is peg strung from a wooden bar inside the head and articulated at the neck, shoulders and hips. Her limbs are long and slender and feet wear moulded two strap shoes and yellow ribbed socks. The bisque is high grade and the decoration exceptional in its muted tones and fine brushwork. Her blue striated eyes are stationary and the long blonde mohair wig is tied with red ribbons at the top. Her low waisted dress and matching bonnet are red sateen with ribbon ties of red silk. Dress is trimmed at the yoke, cuffs and hem with red and white cotton crochet. Underwear is starched gauze and the whole outfit is commercially made.

The doll was bought in Paris in 1900 by Mary Louisa Julian for her daughter Stella who died in 1902. The youngest surviving daughter eventually found it in a drawer still wrapped and presented it to her cousin in whose collection the lovely doll now has pride of place.

Fig 56. 6in (15cm). Peg strung all-bisque girl doll immaculately preserved in her original clothing. (Courtesy Moira Garland)

All-Bisque

Plump toddler

Fig 57. 2¾in (7cm). A plump toddler with chubby cheeks and rounded limbs. A naturalistic face with good modelling and excellent decoration. (Courtesy Jill Lewis)

Fig 57 and 58. During the two decades following the turn of the century, naturalism of doll features took a further step in its course of progress and a realism resulted that was to verge in many instances on caricature. The following two illustrations mark the turning point between the naturalistic — still overlaid with idealism — and the character doll which was uncompromisingly accurate in its portrayal.

Dating to the end of the nineteenth century, the dolls also show a markedly less encumbent style of dress — both wearing little more than shifts. Their dresses and bonnets are home sewn and Fig 58 wears white kid shoes over black moulded boots which have been painted out. Both dolls have articulation at the neck, shoulders and hips and are elastic strung. They have open crown heads with mohair wigs and painted features. In detail, however, the two are quite unalike.

Fig 57 represents a plump toddler with chubby cheeks and rounded limbs. Both hands are modelled as clenched fists and the legs wear white stockings and black ankle boots with heels. 2¾in (7cm) high, the doll has a naturalistic face with good modelling. The decoration also is excellent — large blue painted eyes with black eyelines, dark ochre single stroke eyebrows and lips of light orange. Strong blush marks accentuate the rotundity of her face. The neck of this doll terminates in a bisque loop which supports the elastic passing through to the legs. Her long mohair wig is blonde and cut in a fringe in front. Her clothes mostly of lace are all removable. Lace drawers and a petticoat are held at the waist by drawstrings and a tiny woollen spencer covers the chest. The lace dress is simply made but very effective. The bodice and skirt are in two parts with a wide rouched collar and puffed sleeves to the wrist. Her cream grosgrain bonnet ties beneath the chin and is decorated with two silk rosettes and a pair of feathers.

Girl doll

All-Bisque

Fig 58 is 3½in (9cm) and represents a slightly older girl with longer limbs and a slimmer body. The modelling is again distinctive and the brushwork excellent. Blue painted eyes have a black rim encircling the iris and there are fine black eyelines. The eyes are set wide apart and have intaglio modelling. Eyebrows are light ochre and the lips rose coloured. The neck fits into a kid lined socket and kid washers protect the joints at shoulders and hips. The doll is elastic strung from a wooden bar inside the head. The long blonde mohair wig conceals the numeral 131 incised high on the back of the head.

The doll's slightly bent arms have small hands with fingers and thumbs well defined both on the inner and outer sides. Her legs wear mid-calf socks with a band of blue on top. Traces of her moulded ankle boots show through where the some applied paint has rubbed. Her sleeveless lace dress is made in two sections and is low waisted with a wide collar. A lace petticoat and drawers secured at the waist with drawstrings comprise her undergarments. The lace bonnet is trimmed with pink ribbon at the back and with ribbon loops at the ears.

Fig 58. 3½in (9cm). All bisque with intaglio eyes. She has the numerals 131 incised high on the back of her head. (Courtesy Jill Lewis)

Bibliography

A Concise history of Costume by James Laver.
Thames & Hudson

A History of Womens' Hairstyles 1500-1965 by Jean Keyes
Methuen.

All-Bisque and Half-Bisque Dolls by Genevieve Angione
Nelson.

Costume Cavalcade by Henry Harold Hanson. Methuen.

Encyclopedia of Needlework by Therese de Dillmont
Mulhouse.

English Costume Through the Ages by Joan Clark. English
University Press.

Fashions in Hair by Richard Carson. Peter Owen.

Nineteenth Century English Costume by C Willet
Cunnington and Phyllis Cunnington. Faber & Faber.

Outline of English Costume by Doreen Yarwood. Batsford

The Collectors Encyclopedia of Dolls by Dorothy S,
Elizabeth A, and Evelyn J Coleman. Crown.

The Little Girls' Own Book by Mrs Child (ca 1844).
Chidley.

The Mode in Hats and Headdress by R Turner Wilcox.
Scribners.

The Perfect Lady by C Willet Cunnington. Max Parrish.

The Woman in Fashion by Doris Langley Moore. Batsford

Acknowledgements

Photography

Inside pages
A. C. Cooper
Colin Futcher
Rodney Menzies

Front cover
P.M.S. Productions

Design
Laurie Stewart

Illustration
Diane Tippell

Plate Making and printing
MTA Reproductions Ltd